To Nancy,
best wishes
Sarah Lenton

Backstage at the Opera

Backstage at the Opera

by

Sarah Lenton

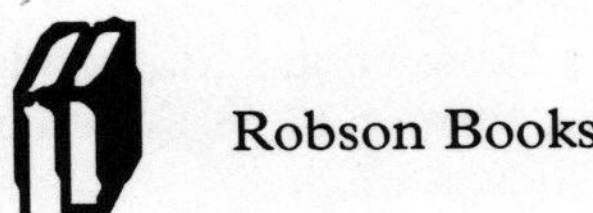

Robson Books

For my parents
Daphne and Trevor Lenton

First published in Great Britain in 1998 by Robson Books Ltd, Bolsover House, 5–6 Clipstone Street, London W1P 8LE

British Library Cataloguing in Publication Data
A catalogue record for this title is available from the British Library

ISBN 1 86105 155 7

The front jacket illustration shows Yvonne Kenny and Christopher Robson in the English National Opera production of *Xerxes*.

Typeset in Plantin by
FSH Print and Production Ltd., London
Printed in Great Britain by St Edmundsbury Press
Bury St Edmunds, Suffolk

Contents

Acknowledgements vii
Foreword ix
Introduction xi
1 Setting the Scene 1
2 Studio Rehearsals 23
3 The Props Department 34
4 The Cactus Run 44
5 The Making Wardrobe 48
6 Enter Nicholas Hytner 55
7 Enter Romilda 59
8 Final Studio Rehearsal 64
9 First Stage-and-Piano Rehearsal 71
10 The Prompt Corner 80
11 Stage and Orchestra 86
12 Wigs and Make-up 94
13 Dress Rehearsal and First Night 97
14 The Running Wardrobe 108
15 Front of House and a Bomb Scare 114
16 The Sound Department 123
17 Quick Changes and the Stage Crew 127
18 The Stage and Crew 134
19 The Sound Box 139
20 The Flys 142
21 Covers 148
22 *Rosenkavalier* 152
23 The Lighting Rig and a Crash 156
24 Lighting 161
25 The Performers 165
26 The Last Night 171
Appendix I: *Opera seria* 176
Appendix II: The Historical Xerxes 185

Acknowledgements

Thanks to . . .

Foreword
by Yvonne Kenny

For those interested in just how an opera is put together, Sarah Lenton has written a fascinating behind the scenes account of rehearsals and performances of Handel's *Xerxes*.

She has explored each aspect of the production process so that we begin to understand the enormous amount of preparation and hard work contributed by the unsung heroes of the opera world; the technical crew, wardrobe, wigs, props, stage crew, electrics, stage management ... as well as those of us up front. We see that a production is team work, everyone depending on everyone else for a successful performance.

So – enjoy this bird's eye view of the world of opera illustrated by Sarah's delightful cartoons. I have been the lucky recipient of several of these as first night cards over the years and they have always succeeded in bringing a welcome smile just at the moment of highest tension.

Yvonne Kenny

Introduction

I spend a great deal of my time guiding people round the London Coliseum and the Royal Opera House. We see the foyers, the Royal Boxes, the dressing rooms and (in limited circumstances) the stage. And, of course, it is the stage in which everybody is interested. As soon as we get anywhere near it the questions start. Where does that rope go to? Who calls the singers? What's it like to sing out there?

After one particularly testing session I decided to do my own crash course on life backstage and I asked Jane Randall, the Stage Manager of English National Opera, if I could shadow her through a show. She very kindly agreed and for the next three months I watched, fascinated, as Handel's opera *Xerxes* took shape in rehearsal.

Of course I didn't just watch; I talked to everybody I met, returning home to thunder their remarks into my computer, and re-appearing the next day to demand corrections – and further explanations. And I was met, at every turn, with patience and generosity from people already burdened with long hours and tight schedules. It is impossible to single out all the members of English National Opera who helped me (though this book could not have been written without them) and I have made what return I can by crediting them whenever they appear in the text and returning them, here, my heartfelt thanks.

Even so, some members of the Company were harrassed more than others and it seems only right to highlight the kindness and patience of Brian Kinsey, Amanda McCaffrey and Lucy Paget as they guided me through the technicalities of stage and sound, and the extraordinary forbearance of the entire *Xerxes* cast who, amongst the stresses of their profession, had presumably never reckoned on tripping over a spare cartoonist in the wings.

Nearer home I am under heavy obligations to the friends who have lived with the book for three years, particularly Margaret

Stonborough and Paul Grist, who read (and re-read) its earlier versions, Philippa Rooke who allowed me to plunder her operatic archives, Jonathan Peter Kenny for his detailed knowledge of *opera seria* and Anne Tennant, probably the fastest proof-reader in the business, certainly the most exact.

1
Setting the Scene

Rehearsals for *Xerxes* began on 13 December at Lilian Baylis House, ENO's studio in West Hampstead, London. I arrived there at 10 a.m. to find that the LBH crew had been at work since 8, hauling out the props and setting them up – they were, at that particular moment, stamping down a grass carpet.

A sturdy rehearsal cake (nothing like the chocolate gateau used in performances) was already on the cake trolley, clearly in readiness for the beginning of Act II, The Coffee House Scene. However, as the plot of *Xerxes* is not well known, I too will set the scene. Readers who have already seen the opera might prefer to join us later on page 23.

The Opera

In 1738 the original *Xerxes* audience was provided with an English translation of the libretto – though its compiler was quick to dismiss any suggestion that he should attempt a synopsis as well. 'The contexture of this Drama,' he wrote on the first page, 'is so very easy, that it wou'd be troubling the reader to give him a very long argument to explain it.' I shall however trouble the reader quite a lot because, though the action is extremely straightforward in the theatre, to follow its staging in the following pages you will need to know the plot rather well – and in its English National Opera dress.

The cast list (see below) plunges us immediately into one of the major difficulties of putting on a Handel opera as the *castrato* voice, the most exciting sound in eighteenth-century opera, no longer exists. Xerxes himself was originally sung by a castrato (a male singer whose unbroken voice has been artificially preserved by castration) and, as the practice of castrating boys for musical careers died out long ago, the ENO was obliged to find an equivalent voice. They made the not uncommon decision of giving the part to a woman mezzo-soprano. The male romantic lead, Arsamenes, was no problem at all as it had been originally sung by

The Cast

XERXES, King of Persia	Mezzo-soprano
ARSAMENES, his brother, in love with Romilda	Countertenor
AMASTRIS, sole heiress to the kingdom of Tagor betrothed to Xerxes and disguised as a man	Mezzo-soprano
ARIODATES, commander of Xerxes' army	Bass
ROMILDA, his daughter, in love with Arsamenes	Soprano
ATALANTA, her sister, secretly in love with Arsamenea	Soprano
ELVIRO, servant to Arsamenes	Bass

a woman anyway (Handel uses the female voice or a high male voice interchangably for practically all his heroes); however, ENO decided they wanted a man in this role, and cast a countertenor.[1] The result of this disposition of parts was very interesting: the aggressive, dominant Xerxes was now played by a woman, and the passive, suffering lover by a man, all of which added a new twist to the normal confusion of gender in an *opera seria*.[2]

Preliminary

The opera is set in ancient Persia. Xerxes, the King, becomes infatuated with Romilda, the daughter of his Commander, Ariodates. Romilda, however, loves and is beloved by Xerxes' brother, Arsamenes, and has no intention of switching her affections. Xerxes responds by banishing Arsamenes (though this does not turn out to be a very serious move as, apart from one scene in exile, Arsamenes drifts dejectedly round the court for the rest of the opera).

The main action of the piece centres round Xerxes' pursuit of Romilda; as an absolute monarch he is in a position to enforce his attentions and Romilda places herself in some danger by rejecting him. However, in the course of the opera Xerxes falls genuinely in love with her and is consequently inhibited from using coercion (though he retains it as an option).

The situation is complicated by two other lovers.

The first is Atalanta, Romilda's younger sister, who fancies herself in love with Arsamenes as well and is determined to win him. Uncluttered by any noticeable scruples she generates enough misinformation to make the lovers thoroughly miserable by the middle of Act II.

The second is Amastris, the fiancée of Xerxes. He supposes her safely at Tagor, of which she is Princess, but she turns up unexpectedly in Persia, providentially in male disguise, and observes his betrayal at first hand. For the rest of the opera she stands apart, barely interacting with the other characters except to pass on messages (she has a useful knack of appearing whenever Xerxes' attentions to Romilda get out of hand).

Two basses complete the cast: Arsamenes' servant Elviro and Ariodates, Xerxes' Commander. It is rare to find a bass in anything other than a supporting role in Handel, and these two are no exception – although Ariodates unwittingly precipitates the denouement and Elviro does his best to stop the plot altogether. Elviro is one of opera's first comic servants, a role he appears to resent.

The ENO Setting

In the English National Opera production Nicholas Hytner, the director, and David Fielding, the designer, set the action in an eighteenth-century vision of Ancient Persia. The result was a clean elegant set in which huge props (such as a large piece of topiary representing an Assyrian bull god) made welcome if slightly baffling appearances. Xerxes himself has obviously been on the Grand Tour and returned with a range of exotic souvenirs, some of which he appears to have picked up in the British Isles. The statue labelled 'Timotheus' is of Handel himself,[3] and the Ancient Persians seem remarkably familiar with the use of deckchairs and umbrellas.

Furthermore, though the characters may be Ancient and Persian, their behaviour is distinctly British; indeed, the inhibitions and levels of embarrassment on stage make it quite clear that, for this show at least, 'Persian' and 'British' are synonymous.

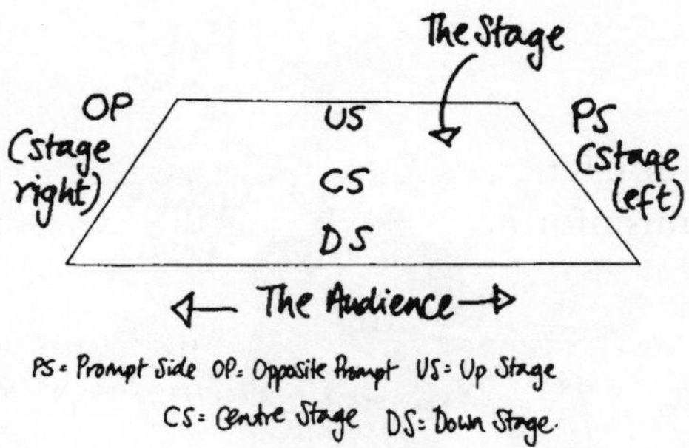

To follow the story line below you will need to learn some simple theatrical compass points:

The Story

Act I

The Concert Scene

During the last section of the Overture the curtain rises on a large eighteenth-century room. Its back walls are covered with a mural of the gardens at Versailles which, spilling over the wainscoting and cornices, leaves one in a pleasant state of uncertainty as to whether one is inside or out. The stage is covered half by a lawn and half by varnished floorboards, a statue of Handel looms above the chorus and, downstage right, a plane tree is standing in a white garden box. (See photo 'Ombra mai fu'.)

Clearly a ceremony is about to take place: the court (dressed and made up in pale grey) watch as a flunky hands Xerxes a silver spade and discreetly applauds as he tips a token handful of earth over the base of the tree. Xerxes sings affectionately to the tree in the *arioso*[4] '*Under thy shade*'[5] and escorts the ladies of the chorus to their seats – green deckchairs which have just been set

up by three impassive flunkeys. (These functionaries are integral to the show and are billed as Wardens on the cast list.) Xerxes sits down – he rates a proper chair – and immerses himself in the programme for the forthcoming concert.

Arsamenes enters unobtrusively downstage, accompanied by his servant Elviro. The brothers are uncannily alike, dressed in full skirted brocade coats, satin Persian trousers and sporting long manes of baroque hair. Arsamenes is keyed up for an assignation with Romilda but fails to enthuse Elviro who a) wants to get back to bed and b) comments that the stage seems rather full for a secret meeting.

Offstage is heard a *sinfonia*,[6] followed by the first lines of Romilda's first song. Everybody stops to listen (except Elviro who grumbles that he can't hear the words) and Romilda makes a diva-like entrance through the twin doors at the back to sing '*Oh hark all ye wounded*'. The *arioso* teases Xerxes for loving a plane tree and causes a mild sensation, but Xerxes is delighted at the attention. He turns to his brother to ask if he knows the singer; Arsamenes hastily says he doesn't. Romilda's next aria '*Swift from the mountains*', is equally well received and she exits pursued by her fans. Xerxes is completely stricken and resolves, aloud, to win her.

There follows a rather fraught recitative[7] between the brothers: Arsamenes points out Romilda's unsuitability both as wife and mistress and categorically refuses to do Xerxes' wooing for him. Xerxes, slightly suspicious of this zeal for the royal good name, closes the discussion with a cheerful aria,[8] '*I will declare my passion*' in which he confidently predicts that his charms will prove irresistible. Arsamenes waits for the King to exit and sings a defiant reprise '*Go, make your declaration*'.

The back wall flies up, revealing a serene blue sky and, upstage, the tiny ruins of ancient Persepolis itself set in a rocky desert. The *scale* of the landscape is left open: it could be a vista of real mountains with the ruins of Persepolis (seen at a vast distance) or a small-scale model laid out in Xerxes' elegant theme park.

Romilda enters upstage, (with her sister Atalanta two steps behind) and Arsamenes pours out his anxiety. Xerxes, he says, wishes to seduce her and, though Romilda reassures him of her constancy, Atalanta comments to the audience that she wishes the King every success. The lovers settle down on some deckchairs downstage and Atalanta sings the aria '*Ah, do not weep*' purporting to be an expression of Romilda's feelings for Arsamenes, though in fact expressing her own. This fools nobody and she leaves in teenage despair.

Elviro, who is seated upstage with a newspaper, suddenly notices the King approaching; he and Arsamenes hide, improbably, behind another couple of deckchairs while Romilda strolls carelessly on the OP grass.

Xerxes approaches Romilda and grandly informs her of her magnificent destiny. To his amazement Romilda temporizes by declaring she is not ambitious; he instantly assumes that Arsamenes has been interfering, an assumption more than confirmed by Arsamenes springing out of hiding to protest. He is promptly banished and he takes his farewell of Romilda in the aria '*Better far, by my departure*' in which distress and reproach (directed at his brother) are nicely balanced. Xerxes' bodyguards, acting in the best traditions of quiet menace, indicate that it is time for Arsamenes to exit and, just as firmly, that Romilda had better stay.

Xerxes moves in, but his insolent confidence provokes nothing but indignation from Romilda. Undeterred, he assails her with the aria '*Who has taught you to disdain me?*' and exits, clearly convinced that he will ultimately carry his point. Romilda is left alone to sing the serene '*No stain shall blemish this constant heart*' leaving us in no doubt of her unshakeable love for Arsamenes.

The Investiture

A vigorous *ritornello*[9] introduces Xerxes' fiancée, Amastris; she enters in a flurry, managing a huge greatcoat and hat and getting her suitcase in everybody's way. Round her the Wardens are setting up for another public ceremony: the deckchairs are re-positioned to face Stage Right and some red ropes are set up to protect an area on the OP; not that one can imagine the beautifully mannered Court ever needing anything as vulgar as crowd control.

Amastris sings a (non *da capo*) aria '*No man's apparel can change what I'm feeling*' to explain that it is love's frenzy that has brought her disguised to Persia and she withdraws to one side as the courtiers enter. They sing a chorus of welcome, '*Now the trumpet's shrill alarm*', to Ariodates who leads on four generals from Downstage Left. An ornate red sofa and knighting stool has appeared in the roped off area, and the king himself waits to greet his commander.

As they cross the stage a huge privet hedge cut in the shape of an Assyrian winged bull rumbles on Upstage Left. Everybody turns, the soldiers freeze and salute and Xerxes looks consciously royal. (See photo 'The Investiture'.) He makes a neat speech praising Ariodates' success in the recent campaign, adding that, as a reward, his daughter Romilda will be given a royal consort equal to Xerxes. The theatre audience is left in no doubt that Xerxes is referring to himself, but it is not so certain that Ariodates understands the King's drift, however he *is* extremely gratified and, in his aria '*I never seek to question*' (during which he and his fellows are knighted), expresses his cheerful co-operation with the Powers That Be.

There is a general exit, leaving only Xerxes and Amastris on stage. She hovers unnoticed behind one of the legs of the Winged God (as it is called on the prop list) and overhears Xerxes' soliloquy. He flatters himself that, having been successful in war, he will be equally fortunate in love, and for a heartbeat, Amastris thinks he is referring to their engagement; however, she is soon disillusioned and his further airy reflections on a King's immunity to criticism infuriate her. She reveals herself by crying out 'Liar!' – and has some difficulty in explaining this remark before Xerxes dismisses her. He has of course not recognized her, for which he has more excuse than people normally have on stage: the hat and coat are very enveloping. (See photo 'Amastris conceals herself'.)

Alone, Xerxes sings the first fully developed *da capo* aria in the opera, '*When I see her, I would hold her,*' a languorous, indulgent meditation on Romilda's charms.

The Hedge Scene

A green drop curtain slowly falls over the scene and *continues* to descend even when it has filled the whole stage. As the top comes into sight, the head and shoulders of a Warden can be seen. He stares impassively at the audience and, just as we begin to realize how very like a hedge the curtain is, he produces a pair of shears and begins to trim it.

Elviro enters with a suitcase and, meeting Arsamenes (kitted out for exile in a full-length greatcoat), is directed to deliver a letter to Romilda. Elviro accepts the job with marked unenthusiasm until, catching his master's eye, he thinks it politic to break out into the hearty arietta[10] '*My lord, my lord, put all your trust in me*'. He exits, along with the Warden who has been radiating disapproval for the whole scene.

Alone on stage Arsamenes sings a pain-filled aria, '*When grief and pain assail me*', and exits, passing Amastris as he does so; both are too miserable to do any more than glower at each other.

THE HERO SENDS A LETTER

Amastris, now dressed as a Persian soldier, rails at Xerxes' treachery and breaks into an impassioned aria, '*Vengeance on him who spurns me*'; she exits overcome with rage and grief.

The Library Scene

(See photo 'The Library Scene'.) The green drop curtain rises on an Interior scene (the same as in Scene 1). The plane tree is now in a glass case and is being studied intently by Romilda, Atalanta and the ladies of the court. Atalanta is soon bored and rouses Romilda, apparently deep in her plane tree information pack, by an ingenuous suggestion that she should swap the exiled Arsamenes for Xerxes. Not noticing the dangerous gleam in Romilda's eye, Atalanta chatters on, maligning Arsamenes' constancy and revealing her *own* willingness to marry him – only to find herself swept down stage and subjected to the full force of a *coloratura*[11] aria '*If you'd seduce him.*' Halfway through the song Romilda's sense of humour reasserts itself and, after making sure that the wretched Atalanta is not let off a single note, she exits magnificently through a phalanx of icy court ladies who have had their quiet morning completely *ruined*.

Left alone on stage, and totally unrepentant, Atalanta ends the act with the aria '*By stealing secret kisses*' – a lively run through of the art of seduction.

Act II

The Coffee Shop

The drop curtain rises on the Interior scene: the Prompt Side is laid out with coffee tables, fenced off from the remainder of the stage by

red ropes. Some of the court are seated at the tables, gravely enjoying coffee and cake, while the rest have formed an orderly queue by the ropes. (See photo 'Coffee Shop'.) The Wardens glide through the scene, ushering people in and out of the Coffee Shop, wheeling cake trolleys and keeping a severe eye on behaviour.

The action in this scene follows quite a formal pattern: a principal enters through the centre doors, sings a tiny *arioso* and gravitates to the Coffee Shop. The first to arrive is Amastris; she sings her *arioso* '*May hope that springs eternal*,' takes an empty table and orders some brandy.

Offstage we hear Elviro singing the first line of his *arioso* '*Ah, who'll buy these flowers?*' and he enters in heavy disguise: a white plastic mac, white plastic hat, and a bag of flowers (which he tries to sell to the queue). In an aside to the audience he pulls off his hat, to astonish us with his real identity, and shows us Arsamenes' letter to Romilda. Amastris (in defiance of all stage convention) overhears him and uses the brandy bottle to lure him to her table. After a couple of sips Elviro has revealed all; he tells Amastris that although the King may love Romilda, *she* loves the exiled Arsamenes. But Amastris' adroit suggestion, that perhaps Arsamenes has given himself solace in exile by writing to Romilda, silences him and he makes a hasty escape.

Her worst suspicions confirmed, Amastris breaks into an impassioned aria, '*Now 'tis plain that the traitor defiles me*,' in the course of which she severely embarrasses the other customers and gets thrown out of the Coffee House; Elviro watches her departure with relief.

Atalanta enters in a wistful mood: '*My fortune has willed me to weep for my hopeless love*.' However, her *arioso* is interrupted by Elviro's flower song and she decides to cheer herself up with a bunch of flowers.

It takes about a second for Elviro to reveal his identity – and errand – and about half a second for Atalanta to offer to deliver his letter to Romilda. Something that could almost be called prudence stirs in Elviro. 'Will she be sure to get it?' he asks and, reassured by a ready 'Yes!' hands it over to Atalanta. She gratuitously adds that Romilda has forgotten Arsamenes anyway and at this moment is writing to Xerxes, a piece of fiction that naturally appalls Elviro. His furious *arietta* '*Ah! viperous evil*' is cut short by the appearance of Xerxes himself and he hurries out. Atalanta wanders over to the Coffee Shop, musing on the best way to capitalise on her acquisition.

Everybody rises as Xerxes enters Upstage and, realizing he is in a reverie, tactfully looks away as he sings the *arioso*, '*He must suffer bitter torment*'. Fortunately the thought of coffee cheers him up and he is ushered to a table. Once there he can hardly help noticing Atalanta, ostentatiously reading Arsamenes' letter, and before he can stop her she has joined his table, given him the letter to read and told him that it has been sent to *her*. (It is important to realize that, due presumably to an excess of caution, Arsamenes has omitted to address the letter to Romilda.) Xerxes is astonished at the news, but does not hesitate to accept Atalanta's glib explanation that Arsamenes has simply been *pretending* to love Romilda so that he can actually woo Atalanta undisturbed.

The two form an alliance. Xerxes promises to insist that Arsamenes marry Atalanta and, well pleased with the way things are going, prepares to eat a slice of chocolate cake. He is not fated to eat it. Atalanta, heedless of Persian etiquette, launches into an aria, '*He'll say that love for me ne'er stabbed his aching heart*,' in which she tries to forestall Arsamenes' inevitable objections when he learns of his matrimonial future. Xerxes listens politely, but is sorely tried when she sings the whole aria again a minute later. He eventually manages to dismiss her, having first secured the letter which he intends to show to Romilda.

During Atalanta's reprise, the Wardens have cleared away the Coffee Shop and, as she exits, the back wall flies up to reveal all of them, in gardening aprons, holding enormous potted cactuses which they place at regular intervals across the stage.

The Cactus Scene

Romilda appears Downstage Left, with a couple of companions, obviously hoping to find half an hour's solace amidst the royal cactus collection. A few ladies are already studying the plants with the aid of a handsomely printed leaflet.

Xerxes approaches and, with a decent show of solicitude, hands her Arsamenes' letter. Romilda recognizes her lover's handwriting and (in the only illogical moment in the plot) reads it with composure, only asking to whom it is addressed once she has got to the end.[12] Xerxes replies that it was sent by Arsamenes to Atalanta.

Romilda retreats into herself in agony, a reaction that baffles Xerxes who has naively expected her to fall into his arms. They sing a short duet (just 18 bars) in which Romilda counters Xerxes' persistent '*Will you love him?*' with an unswerving '*Evermore!*', and a furious *allegro ritornello* launches Xerxes into his next aria, '*If you'd worship the man who has spurn'd you, I'd renounce you.*' The director, Nick Hytner, clearly saw a touch of parody in this outburst, though the King's swings into an *adagio* phrase, ' – *but truly, I cannot*' are genuine enough.

Romilda, unnerved by all this energy, puts a couple of cactuses between herself and the King – who immediately dodges round them – and the aria is punctuated from then on by an agitated chase round the stage. By the end, however, Romilda's innate self-possesion has re-asserted itself, and Xerxes, inhibited for the first time in his life by sincere emotion, finds

he cannot reach her. He exits in bewilderment.

Left alone, Romilda gives way to resentment; she denounces her sister and lover in an accompanied recitative,[13] following this with the pain-filled aria, '*That ruthless tyrant jealousy racks me.*'

She exits just as Amastris stumbles on, holding a dagger before her and threatening to kill herself. Fortunately, Elviro has also entered; he rapidly removes the dagger and suggests she should concentrate more on food and drink, particularly drink. Amastris hardly hears him as she breaks into a passionate *arioso* in which she begs the absent king to kill her: '*As you betray me, there's naught to live for*'.

She too exits and Elviro is just dismissing her as a passing nutter when he is brought up by the appearance of Arsamenes. Reluctantly, he passes on Atalanta's story, that Romilda now loves the King, and leaves his master to pour out his distress in a *da capo* '*Once we would kiss and play.*'

The Storm Scene

In spite of the fact that the sky has been darkening since Xerxes' last aria, the chorus enter in a cheerful mood singing a jaunty *coro*[14] and admiring a small model bridge which has just been wheeled on. The Wardens swiftly strike[15] the cactuses and Xerxes enters (with Ariodates) deep in a blueprint of a bridge that he hopes will span the Hellespont. After a sketchy description of his projected European campaign, Xerxes dismisses both Ariodates and the chorus who exit singing his praises.

A mournful *arioso*, '*Must my days be spent lamenting?*' heralds the arrival of the unfortunate Arsamenes to whom Xerxes, convinced that he really loves Atalanta, now wishes to be reconciled. He rallies Arsamenes on his secret love and gives him permission to marry. Arsamenes is amazed but sensibly closes with the offer, only realising they have been talking at cross-purposes when Xerxes reveals *his* plans for the double wedding: he will be married to Romilda, and Arsamenes to Atalanta.

Goaded beyond the limits of Persian etiquette (and *opera seria* convention), Arsamenes bursts, without *ritornello*, into the *da capo*

'*Yes, I want her!*' (the 'her', of course, being Romilda). This energetic number brilliantly interupts the sequence of suffering arias that Arsamenes has been singing for most of the show. His fury sweeps all before him and he storms out, leaving Xerxes indignant and speechless. (See photo 'Arsamenes snaps'.)

Unfortunately Atalanta chooses this moment to see how things are going and she enters to find the King in a spiteful mood. He tells her peremptorily that Arsamenes does not love her and that she should instantly forget him; only to find Atalanta reminding *him*, in her aria '*You advise me to forget him*,' that one cannot control one's heart so easily. This brings all Xerxes' latent anxiety to the surface and he describes his own sufferings in an extended *da capo*, '*The heart that love has captured*'.

The sky is now almost black and all sensible characters have retired but Elviro, anxious to find his master – and fortified by his hip flask – comes on stage and improbably examines the tiny bridge to see if Arsamenes is lurking near it. The storm breaks, thunder rolls, the rain comes down and a bolt of lightning destroys the bridge. Elviro looks nervously at the wreckage and decides to retire, though not before he has expressed his general dislike of water in a drinking song, '*If my dearest wish were granted me*.'

The Pillar Scene

The rain peters out as some Wardens enter to wheel off the bridge and five pillar bases begin to descend from the flys.[16] For a moment we assume that we are to be treated to five Babylonian columns but it shortly becomes apparent that only one of the pillars is complete.

Xerxes enters Downstage, unaware that Amastris has also entered and is hiding behind the whole pillar. He unwittingly sings a duet with her, his line, '*A jealous fiend has snared me*,' being answered by her, '*That same affliction burns me*'. They continue like this for several bars until Amastris' feelings get the better of her. Her cry, '*Stony-hearted Xerxes!*', is overheard by the King who immediately institutes inquiries.

She pretends to be a veteran, neglected by the King, and her recital of the injuries she has received is loaded with dramatic irony. Xerxes is naturally oblivious of double meanings and vaguely promises redress, and dismisses her hastily as Romilda enters (apparently under guard).

He has clearly decided to sidestep the hesitation of his last aria and, approaching Romilda with a curious mixture of wheedling and impudence, offers her a gift of jewellery. Remarkably, Romilda hesitates. She does after all think that Arsamenes is unfaithful but the realisation that Xerxes is trying to *buy* her is decisive and, snapping the jewel box shut, she returns his present with the aria, '*The heart that beats contented*.'

Xerxes is beside himself and demands she accepts him on the spot. Romilda, caught between him and his guards, is in a tricky position but, luckily, Amastris rushes on, sword drawn, urging her to refuse him. Xerxes orders 'his' instant arrest and, fortunately, stalks off while Romilda airily countermands the order. The guards, presumably unsure of her exact status, withdraw. Amastris too retires, remarking darkly that it was not merely on Romilda's account that she has saved her.

Romilda dismisses the incident from her mind and, in a change of mood typical of Handel heroines at the end of Act II, decides to cheer up. The sky, it is true, is still dark; the ladies of the chorus have just entered with their umbrellas; Arsamenes is unfaithful and the king decidedly dangerous – but a faithful heart will surely triumph. She sings a radiant aria '*The love cross'd by fortune*' and, as she reaches the *da capo*, the ladies lower their umbrellas to applaud her as a rainbow appears in the sky.

Act III

The Egg Scene

The Act opens with a gigantic Egg being parked downstage in front of the Hedge Curtain. It is clearly part of the Royal collection and is guarded by an impassive Warden. As the orchestra plays a *sinfonia*, the hedge rises to head height and we see the cast sitting in deckchairs and deep in '*The Inquirer*' – a Persian newspaper, set in impeccable classic type. (See photo 'Newspaper Scene'.)

The Egg is solemnly wheeled across the stage, attracting everybody's attention except Arsamenes and Romilda who, flanking Elviro in the centre of the row, are both convinced of the other's unfaithfulness. They read their newspapers *at* each other,

to Elviro's acute embarrasment, and he begs Atalanta (who wanders on downstage, and then clearly wishes she hadn't) to explain the story she told him in Act II. Atalanta says, rather lamely, that she made the whole thing up to protect the lovers from Elviro's indiscretion – and has the mortification of seeing them immediately reconciled. She sings an aria of miserable defiance, '*No, no, though you detest me*', before she exits.

However, Romilda and Arsamenes have barely time to hold

hands before they are warned by Elviro that the king is approaching; Arsamenes dodges swiftly behind a huge griffin head as his brother strides in with his guards in attendance. Xerxes has clearly had enough of civilised courtship and demands that Romilda should accept him immediately. The hapless Romilda (penned on the central deck chair between the guards) temporises as best she can, by insisting that her father should be asked for his consent, but finds it impossible to actually disobey her king. Utterly indifferent to her obvious distress, Xerxes exits with a cheerful aria, '*I go in certain hope*', leaving her to face the wrath of Arsamenes, who bursts out of hiding to reproach her with unfaithfulness and ambition. Romilda, quite overcome by her misfortunes, exits without the customary aria and Arsamenes pours out his grief in a *da capo* '*Ah love, tyrannic love*' before he too leaves the stage.

The Bowling Scene

The back wall flies up and a couple of palm trees, set on the OP upstage, indicate that we are out in the open again. The Generals enter, each of them holding a bowl, and they throw a white jack along the grass carpet as they wait for Ariodates to finish a confidential recitative with Xerxes downstage. Xerxes is, of course, obtaining Ariodates' consent to his marriage with Romilda but, as he still insists on referring to himself obliquely (as '*a man of royal blood, who is our equal*'), Ariodates' confusion as to who this mysterious person might be is very understandable. He eventually comes to the conclusion that the king must be referring to *Arsamenes* and Xerxes leaves, unaware that his Commander has got hold of the wrong end of the stick. Ariodates sings a *da capo* '*Who'd have expected such an achievement?*' while he and the Generals celebrate the proposed marriage with a game of bowls. They exit just as Romilda enters, her nerve recovered and her mind made up to refuse the king.

However, *his* jubilant entrance two seconds later rather throws her and she tries to get out of the engagement indirectly by revealing that Arsamenes once kissed her. Unfortunately this only succeeds in exasperating Xerxes who, summoning his guard, orders Arsamenes' immediate execution, and leaves in a rage – just as Amastris makes another of her providential entries.

In a hurried recitative Romilda pours out her troubles and secures Amastris' promise to find Arsamenes and warn him of his danger; Amastris asks her, in return, to deliver a letter to the King. Romilda runs off and Amastris reflects that much of her *own* misery is self-inflicted ('*I am the cause of my own ruin*').

Arsamenes enters as this *arioso* ends and his whispered conversation with Amastris upstage is designed to convince us that she is warning him of Xerxes' threat. (There is no recitative written for this encounter; the original librettist presumably assumed she could hiss him a warning as they passed in the wings.) Be that as it may, Arsamenes is now in a state as unreasonable as his brother and totally convinced that Romilda is unfaithful. Her her entrance downstage, as Amastris leaves, is the cue for him to load her with accusations. Why has she sent a message? There isn't a plot at all! She simply wants an excuse to leave him. The tirade is only cut short by a mighty slap, administered by the much put-upon Romilda, and the two settle down to have a blazing row, ('*You insult a constant lover*').

The Quarrel Duet, as it is called at ENO, is a show-stopper; its driving energy neatly undercut by the staging, which suggests that one of the lovers at least (Arsamenes) is rather taken aback at the fury he has unleashed. At the end of the 'A' section Romilda storms off PS with Arsamenes, after a rueful glance at the audience, two steps behind. The Hedge Curtain comes in and, as the *ritornello* pounds on and the audience are wondering whether to clap, Romilda marches in again – from the opposite side – with her lover right behind. The middle section and the *da capo* are thick with recriminations and the duet ends with Romilda leaving via PS again, this time for good.

The Bust Scene

The Hedge Curtain flies up to reveal Ariodates and the Court, standing in formal rows amongst a row of royal busts, and singing a chorus about the inevitability of Fate, '*All things human must decay*'. This must be assumed to be a Persian wedding hymn. Ariodates is certainly all set to marry the lovers and is delighted when they appear. Romilda and Arsamenes enter in a burst of recitative – the last rumble of their quarrel – but Ariodates' revelation that Xerxes intends them to marry changes everything. Instant harmony reigns, Ariodates joins their hands and, sending them off to thank the King, joins the Court in another suitable chorus, '*Desolation turns to bliss*'. (See photo 'The Wedding Scene'.)

Everybody leaves as Xerxes enters downstage, dressed in cloth of gold; he has at last determined to tell Ariodates exactly *who* the royal bridegroom is and hails the Commander affably as he re-enters. The two men talk at cross-purposes for a bar or two, but Ariodates' revelation that Romilda is offstage with her *husband* naturally provokes a bout of panic stricken questioning and brings the whole pack of cards down on his unlucky head.

Xerxes' rage is temporally arrested by a Warden entering with a letter, ostensibly from Romilda. Ariodates is ordered to read it, a job he does not appear to relish – especially as the letter, starting off '*Most ungrateful of all lovers*' and continuing in this reproachful strain, does little to appease Xerxes' fury. The signature, however, alters everything; it is signed 'Amastris'. Utterly humilated, Xerxes orders Ariodates from the stage and explodes into his *coloratura* aria '*Rise, ye furies from baleful abysses!*' Though the furious pace of the music and the brilliant runs in the vocal line vividly convey the King's rage, there is a hint of parody about the piece that suggests that all this passion might not be far removed from a temper tantrum. (A suspicion reinforced in the ENO staging: Xerxes hurls down the busts of his ancestors in the *da capo* – where they smash very satisfactorily on the grass).

The wedding party re-enters and Xerxes, now beside himself, draws his sword and insists that Arsamenes kill Romilda with it, there and then. Amastris enters and (ignoring Xerxes' understandable, 'Who are you, who yet *again* interrupts me?') asks him if he really wants to see a faithless heart pierced by one who loves it. 'Yes!' says Xerxes. Amastris snatches the sword and points it at him. He must die then. He is the traitor and she, at last revealing her identity, is his faithful Amastris. Xerxes is overwhelmed, embarrassed and, possibly, even penitent. He asks her if she can still love him and, being assured of her forgiveness, asks everybody's pardon as he reluctantly releases Romilda to Arsamenes.

The last aria is Romilda's (the tender '*Sweetest and best of lovers*') after which the principals close the opera with the *coro*, '*So love bestows its blessing*'. As they sing, the lovers take centre stage, oblivious of everything except their own happiness, while Xerxes, turning from Amastris' embrace, regards them wistfully.

Notes

1 A singer with a normal male voice who sings in the high part of his range – the *falsetto*.

2 *Opera seria* ('serious opera') was the usual form for an Italian opera in the eighteenth century and worked to a specific set of rules. Handel was clearly happy to work in this framework and his operas are all *opere serie*; however, the rules sit very lightly on *Xerxes*. *Opera seria* is described more fully in Appendix 1 on page 176.

3 Timotheus was the court musician to Alexander the Great and sang at a feast in Persepolis to celebrate Alexander's victory over Xerxes' descendant, Darius.

4 An *arioso* is a brief 'one mood' aria.

5 The words in Italian are '*Ombra mai fu*' and the *arioso*, known in the nineteenth century as Handel's *Largo*, is often considered to be the hit tune of the opera.
6 A short orchestral passage (here played by an offstage band).
7 Recitative is the lightly scored part of the opera in which the plot develops. The characters converse in musical lines that are based on natural speech rhythms.
8 This aria is in *da capo* form. See Appendix for a full description of the convention. Here it is just necessary to know that a *da capo* is an aria in three parts: the first music 'A', second music 'B', and 3, a repeat of 'A'. The singer usually ornaments the repeated 'A'. All arias in *Xerxes* are *da capo* unless otherwise stated.
9 An orchestral passage that opens and closes an aria, usually associated with the 'A' tune of a *da capo*.
10 This is a lyrical outburst, even shorter than an *arioso*.
11 A brilliant, highly ornamented aria.
12 One would expect her to assume it was addressed to her; if she thought for a moment it was *not* she would surely go up the wall immediately.
13 Most recitative is accompanied by a handful of instruments, a harpsichord (usually) joined sometimes by a double bass, cello, bassoon or theorbo. However, Handel sometimes highlights a particularly dramatic recitative by adding the full orchestra. This is called an *accompanied* recitative.
14 *Coro* is Italian for 'chorus', meaning both the performers *and* the music they sing.
15 Props or scenery are 'struck' when they are removed from the stage.
16 The area above the stage into which cloths, flat scenery, props, and lighting bars are 'flown'.

2

Studio Rehearsals

December 13th. Back to Lilian Baylis House for the first rehearsal

LBH (as it is inevitably called) is arranged over three floors. The wardrobe occupies most of the top floor, rehearsal studios and coaching rooms account for the ground floor while the crew, the archives and some mice live in the basement. ENO usually has several shows in rehearsal at the same time and *Xerxes* found itself sharing LBH with a new production of *Der Rosenkavalier*. The latter's huge cast and massive scenery was naturally installed in Studio 3 (that boasts an acreage similar to the Coliseum stage) which left Studio 1 for *Xerxes*. The smallest studio, number 2 is so small that it is used only for music coaching or dance warm-ups; however, Studio 1 is not exactly a prairie, and there were times when it seemed rather a tight fit.

The LBH crew were just stacking the cactuses on a platform as I arrived and, looking round at the available space, I thought it would be prudent to join them. One of the crew, Lawrence Rafferty, chatted about the LBH Christmas party as he tossed cactuses. 'I'm going to put most of *Xerxes* away,' he said, 'except the cactuses. We're going to wind Christmas tree lights round them . . .'

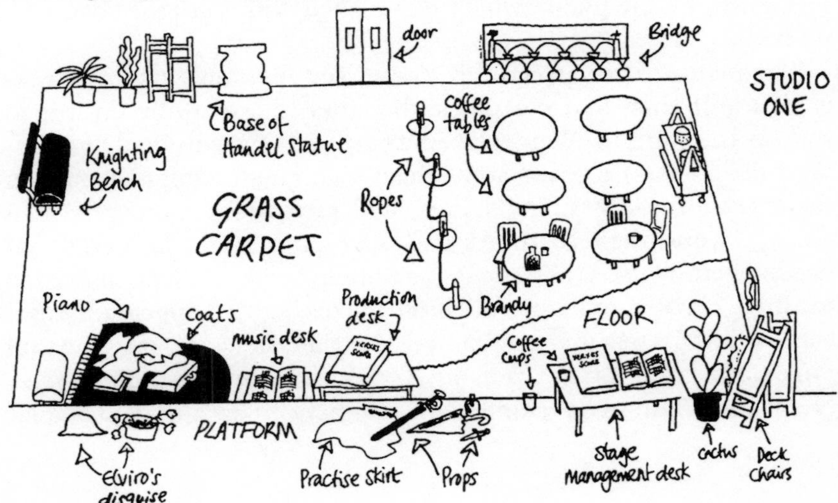

On the studio floor Jane Randall (the Stage Manager) was being less enthusiastic about the props as she inspected the faded grass carpet.

'It looks like Centre Court at the end of Wimbledon,' she said gloomily. Her stage management desk was also up on the platform (amongst the cactuses) and overlooking the music and production desks. Emma Jenkins (the producer's assistant) was already at the latter, steadily going through this morning's scenes in the Production Book.

Every opera generates its own set of books.[1] The Wardrobe Book, for example, which itemises every piece of costume (and its care), the Stage Management Book, marked up with all the cues, and the Production Book which details the basic moves. Emma was looking up the action in the Coffee House Scene, not simply to prompt the singers but to remind herself of what went on; no chorus or actors had been 'called' for this rehearsal and she could expect to be playing Everybody Else.

By 10.30 everybody called for the first session had arrived and packed themselves somewhere round the perimeter of the studio. Julia Hollander, the revival producer, and Emma were on the production desk; Noel Davis, the assistant conductor, beat time from the music desk, Brenda Hurley, the repetiteur,[2] was, naturally, at the piano; and the stage management team, Jane Randall, Nicole Richardson and Bob Pagett, were either sitting up in their eyrie or prowling round the floor checking out chairs and props. The singers perched where they could (though their natural centre of gravity seemed to be the piano, which was loaded with outdoor coats and scores).

The platform was piled with *Xerxes* paraphernalia: swords, deck-chairs, umbrellas and costumes, the latter in a fearfully un-ironed state as the Running Wardrobe (the part of the Wardrobe that maintains the clothes) is based at the theatre and hadn't got its hands on them yet. Louise Winter (Xerxes) and Jean Rigby (Amastris) had already found their costumes and were putting on the items that needed getting used to (basically swords and jackets). Jean discarded the huge black overcoat in which she makes her first appearance as it was without its belt and unwearable. ('It was always too big,' she said philosophically.) Louise put on Xerxes' jacket, gloves and shoes, Nerys Jones (Atalanta) climbed into a practice skirt and Paul Napier

Burrows (Elviro) disappeared into his mac. The crew finished stabilising a wobbly coffee table, and the first rehearsal was ready to go.

I was of course used to seeing rehearsals on the Coliseum stage and was unprepared for the intimacy of the studio. The production team was standing right next to Noel (amiably beating time with a pencil) and only a couple of feet away from the singers. We started with Elviro's first entrance in Act II. Paul was new to his role and he began by pacing out the scene (stalked by Emma) while he spoke the recitative and talked through the subtext with Julia.

Subtext describes the thoughts and feelings that are presumed to be going through the character's head when on stage. It is teased out from the score and libretto in an effort to understand the character and provide an explanation for various activities, whether they turn out to be solidly heroic or confined to opening and shutting doors. A great deal of time is spent in new productions establishing the subtext and, when the show is revived, the producer has to re-activate it for a newcomer.

In this scene both Julia and Noel dug into their memories to remember why Elviro, normally the 'Eeyore' of the opera, enters so cheerfully at the start of Act II and why he should make his sententious remark that, though a commoner is all right for a *mistress*, a King should marry a princess.

'This is the first time you're without Arsamenes,' said Julia, apropos of the first point, 'you feel as though you've been let out of a cage.'

'I remember Nick saying you were a working class Tory,' said Noel, addressing the second.

Paul, however, seemed more baffled by the plastic carnations he was supposed to be selling (his *arioso* describes his wares as honeysuckle, nodding violets and roses). 'I suppose these become violets, roses and all that,' he said, looking at them dubiously.

'Oh no, they are *all* carnations' Julia said. 'You are such a good salesman you can sell them as anything.'

'You do get fresh ones on the night,' she added.

Paul walked the scene again with a phalanx of people round him.

It was time for Jean Rigby to join us and the rehearsal moved into another gear. She had sung Amastris in the original 1985 run (and most of the subsequent revivals) and her performance was, of course, so accurate that rehearsing her turned out to be mostly a matter of establishing which table she sat at and what direction her brandy was supposed to come from. There was a lacuna in the Production Book at this point, but Jean's automatic glance PS settled the point immediately.

She used the brandy decanter to tempt Elviro into the Coffee House and encourage him, between gulps, to tell her everything he knew about the switch in Xerxes' affections. Julia stopped to muse as to why the scene happens at all.

'She doesn't *need* to pump Elviro, she knows all this,' she said.

'Ah,' said Jean, 'she's twisting the knife in the wound . . .' A remark that shed a ray of light on the shameless self pity of her subsequent aria '*Now 'tis plain that the traitor defiles me'*.

We skipped the aria, however, and Jean joined me on the platform. I said that was the first I knew it was brandy Amastris called for. 'Oh yes, it's apple juice.' said Jean, which only made sense when I learned later that though ENO serves up apple juice for brandy, burnt sugar water is usually used for whisky, whisky (especially the Red Label used in *Madame Butterfly*) being a darker brown.

Meanwhile Nerys and Paul were being taken through the next bit of recitative, in which Atalanta secures Arsamenes' letter to Romilda and calmly sets about blackening her sister's character in the process. Nerys, also new to her role, was working from the scanty cues written into her vocal score, and simply walked the scene; Julia joined her on the studio floor to talk through the subtext.

'You haven't got the lies about Romilda ready worked out,' she said, 'you're experimenting.'

'OK,' said Nerys, 'I'm making up the story – I don't know where it's going . . .' and, to my amazement, as she spoke the recitative with this in mind, each lie came out new minted. '*Lock'd in her private chamber/ writing to the King/that she loves him/and will have him*' and then, pursuing her subtext, 'Then I get this letter and I think "How am I going to use this?" '

Nerys became so absorbed that she was still scanning the letter when Elviro asked indignantly about Arsamenes, and her airy '*Oh, he has been quite forgotten*' *was so natural that it prompted Paul's furious arietta and exit; as he stomp*ed off he flung his flower bag down on the piano and I noticed that the Props department makes sure that the letter doesn't manage to lose itself amongst the carnations.

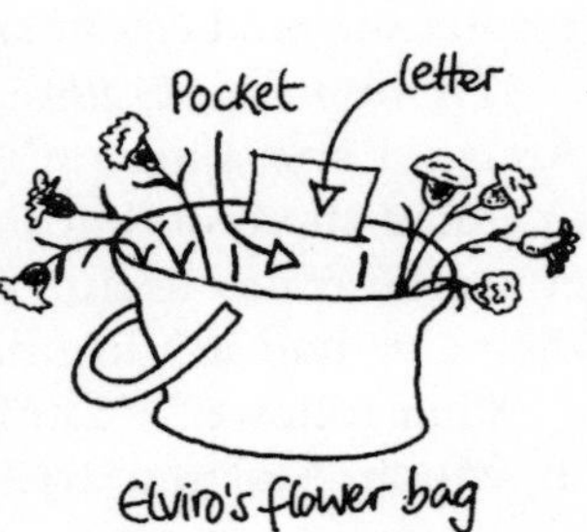

All this of course was leading up to the pivotal scene in which Atalanta seriously misleads Xerxes, and sets up the whole action of Act II. The rest of the session was devoted to it.

As Louise took the floor the mood of the rehearsal shifted again; here was a performer who had sung the part three times on stage, understudied Ann Murray, and was now about to make the role her own. She entered with Xerxes' *arioso* '*He must suffer bitter torment*' and talked through her encounter with Atalanta in an energetic mix of recitative and subtext.

'So I have this little moment of melancholy (the *arioso*). I'm luxuriating really. Then I move off to the Coffee House, very pleased with myself. I get some coffee. What next? Ah, food!' (Emma wheeled the cake trolley past.) 'And now all I need is – Goodness me, what a pretty girl!' (noticing Nerys, ostentatiously reading Arsamenes' letter) '*May I ask of you, madam, what is contained in that letter? Does some gentleman love you?* – It's a pick up, isn't it? Reverie, food, sex. Its all very chappish.'

Julia joined them amongst the coffee tables. 'This scene is about space,' she said. 'Atalanta keeps breaking Persian[3] etiquette by invading the King's space; the less sophisticated characters don't know how to respond to the tight etiquette of the Coffee House.'

They ran the scene, Nerys following the moves recorded in the

Production Book. (See illustrations 1 and 2.) As you can see they accurately record the stage action but they give no impression of the way that Atalanta darts at the king, hovers round him, and darts in again. 'She's like a little wasp,' said Louise.

Louise talked the scene through a couple of times before she sung a note; she read Arsamenes' letter, and embellished as she went.

'*Tis from my brother*. Damn! Him again. Then I realise that Atalanta and I are on the same side. I remember Ann (Murray) changed the mood at this moment to complicity. Hmm, Atalanta could be quite useful. Do sit down (motioning to Nerys) – and then I've had it! Give her an inch . . .'

What followed was of course the aria '*He'll say that love for me*', in which Atalanta tries to make sure that Arsamenes' natural objections to marrying her are not allowed to deflect the king from insisting on it. She also successfully frustrates all Xerxes' attempts to eat a slice of chocolate cake; this is no great hardship in rehearsal as the cake provided by stage management had obviously been chosen for its durable qualities (the chocolate gateau used in the show was quite another matter).

'OK,' said Louise eventually, 'I give up on the cake,' and, standing up, indicated that Atalanta should retire a few paces. She began to stride offstage.

'Head down, Louise!' cried Julia, 'the famous Xerxes stomp.'

'Oh, of course,' said Louise, '*he* never has to worry that anybody'll get in his way.'

However, Atalanta did block the king's path as she sang her aria again, and Louise was forced to stop, which she did irresolutely; Xerxes, we gathered, was quite at a loss when confronted with such natural behaviour.

Nerys was told to go over the top in her last flurry of notes.

'Go down to the footlights,' said Julia.

'Make the most of it,' said Noel.

With this encouragement, her last phrase was delivered and in ringing tones. Louise looked at her thoughtfully. 'You could steal the show,' she said.

Noel looked up to warn Nerys about a bit of the aria where she wouldn't be able to see the beat and then sort of flapped his left hand

Noel demonstrates how to decorate

as he sung the last couple of phrases. Nerys looked completely blank.

'That means decorate,' said Noel.

'When he does that,' said Louise, 'he actually means make it up.'

On this helpful note the session ended.

December 14th. The chorus and actors arrive.

Xerxes, unlike most Handel operas, demands the services of a real chorus; there are three ensembles for Xerxes' admiring subjects and Nicholas Hytner was accordingly provided with the services of the ENO chorus. They are of course Xerxes' court and Hytner added them to any scene that seemed to require an audience whether they sang or not. Smaller groups, however, were played by actors and actresses; the latter usually in attendance on Romilda, and the former turning up as Wardens, waiters or Xerxes' bodyguards. In their darker moments the actors were inclined to growl that they were there just there to shift things but there are several moments in the opera when they steal the show – a fact brought home to me by a conversation that rumbled down the ground floor corridor before rehearsal.

1st Actor: 'Are you pushing the Egg this time, Derek?'

2nd Actor: (Derek presumably) 'Oh, I dunno.'

1st Actor: 'We'll have to fight for that because I used to push the Egg . . .'

Another Actor (diplomatically): 'Who's cutting the Hedge?'

All the actors, actresses and chorus had been called for the first session and by 10.30 the studio (set for the Concert Scene) was covered with people perched on every possible surface and, apparently, talking at the top of their voices. Two ladies beside me immediately disappeared into deck chairs.

'Let's hope we do lots of this scene,' said one.

'I love this show,' said the other.

Jane called for quiet (one of her major activities in that session) and Julia introduced all the principals, particularly Christopher Robson (Arsamenes) who had been called for the first time, and Sally Harrison, covering[4] for Romilda (Yvonne Kenny) who was singing in Melbourne at that moment and would be arriving later.

During a rehearsal period covers lead a rather restricted life, shadowing their principal and rehearsing in the Balcony Bar at the Coliseum, so the chance to work in a main rehearsal must have been quite welcome. However, Sally had apparently not had any calls yet and I wondered if the prospect daunted her.

Julia reminded the chorus of the context of their world, 'You live a half life,' she said, 'your movements are poised, articulated, elegant *and done at half speed*.' The chorus picked up their concert programmes and walking sticks and Louise sang her opening number to the Plane Tree, '*Under thy shade*'.

'I fancy myself at Public Speaking,' she said, 'This is something I do really well.'

She turned with mock modesty to the court and was greeted with noiseless clapping. There was the slightest confusion as to which ladies she escorted to their seats but the chorus clearly knew the show very well. Emma and the Book were hardly referred to at all and Julia concentrated on fine-tuning their reactions. 'There should be a ripple when Romilda first mentions the King. She's being cheeky about him – it's rather exciting,' she said.

Sally Harrison sang the concert aria '*Swift from the mountains*' with extraordinary aplomb while Julia hastily blocked in her arm movements from the production desk since the chorus have to applaud at the final flick.

Yesterday's interest in subtext went by the board as the main focus of interest switched from the characters' motivation to the mechanics of moving a large group effortlessly round the stage ('Float offstage after your curtsey,' said Julia to the chorus ladies) and the smooth running of the action. The actors practised bringing on the deck chairs two at a time, setting them up with

the curious *Xerxes* glide, and Jane Randall and her team were much more evident on the floor, edging along the 'wings' (the sides of the studio) as they dished out programmes, cued people on, or handed out props. The Tree had its own litter to carry it off stage and the Investiture ropes were set with a special sideways walk that had to be rehearsed over and over again.

Props suddenly leapt into prominence. Xerxes' gloves was brought on by an actor, Amastris' suitcase was taken off by an actor and the knighting sword used to knight Xerxes' generals was carried on on its own cushion. The Bridge Scene naturally featured the Bridge, as well as Ariodates' blueprint of the same and it was here that I learnt that props on stage are as near the real thing as possible. The plan of the Bridge was just that (and very neat too, see illustration 9b), the letters were written out verbatim and the various programmes were remarkable pastiches of eighteenth century catalogues (illustration 20).

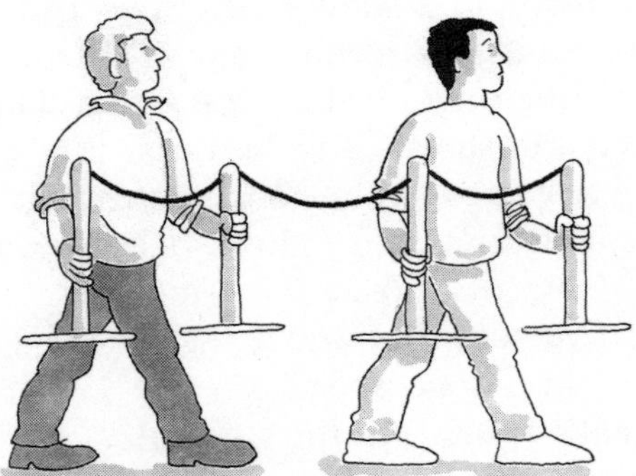

The only things not in evidence were the cactuses. However, at the end of the afternoon Lawrence and his mates were summoned to set them up for the Cactus Scene. They hauled the plants (which appear to be indestructible) off the platform and, following the numbers chalked on their backs, set them up in a grid over the studio floor. Number 12 had a small hollow pipe stuck in the earth at the back for Elviro to shove Amastris' dagger into when she isn't looking.

The scene was run essentially for the actors. The Wardens are discovered at the beginning of the Cactus Scene ranged in solemn rows upstage, each holding a cactus. In the brief time it takes to play the spread chord that heralds Xerxes' recitative '*Poor deluded Romilda!*', they set them in a grid across the stage and exit. Romilda meanwhile has made her entrance downstage left.

Julia dished out the cactuses – the tallest actor inevitably getting the tallest cactus – and gave the most experienced Wardens the job of setting the two DS plants. As there are only 10 actors and 12 cactuses, the DS pair have to be brought in (with dignified haste) from the wings *after* the others have been set. They rehearsed the scene in real time, that is from the time they grab the cactus backstage (during the last *ritornello* of Atalanta's '*He'll say that love for me*') to the moment Jane Randall warns them (*sotto voce*) that the cloth in front of them is flying out. They also have to get into their gardening aprons but this detail was added later.

There are moments in a show that always provoke a clap and the inspired silliness of this scene is one of them.

'There's more time to enter than you think,' said Noel to Sally (who hadn't seen the show), and he burst into a round of solo applause to help her pace her entrance downstage.

Striking the cactuses is even tighter. It is done in the *ritornello* of the chorus '*Long live Xerxes!*' (something like five seconds) and has to be done at super speed which is especially tough on the two actors who have to strike the two extra cactuses as well. Julia said anxiously, 'Could we have *fast* half-life here?'

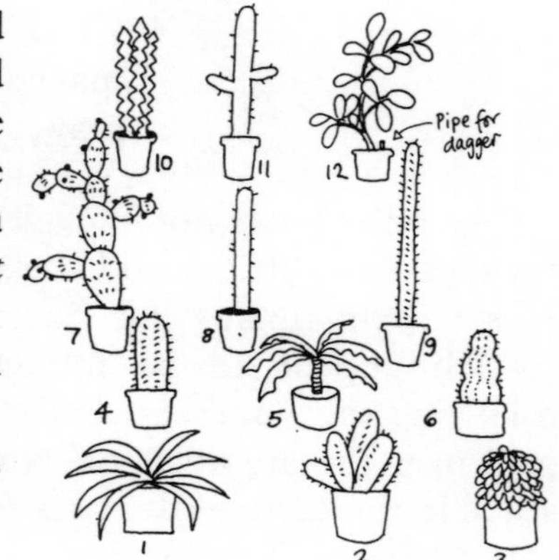

'Ah,' said one of the actors, 'you mean scene-change life.'

'Ye—es,' said Julia, 'but with economy of movement . . .'

After a couple of gallops, the cactuses started to get set and struck with something approaching faultless elegance but I didn't realise until we got to the theatre how approximate this sort of thing is. There was no way Julia could reproduce the dash through the wings (in the dark) and the rapid formation behind the cloth at the beginning of the scene – or the frantic hurling of cactuses to the prop staff at the end. However, even in the civilised conditions prevailing at LBH, it was obvious that the cactuses led a very tough life indeed, and as their construction and continued existence was something of a puzzle, I decided to take a day off to visit the Props Department.

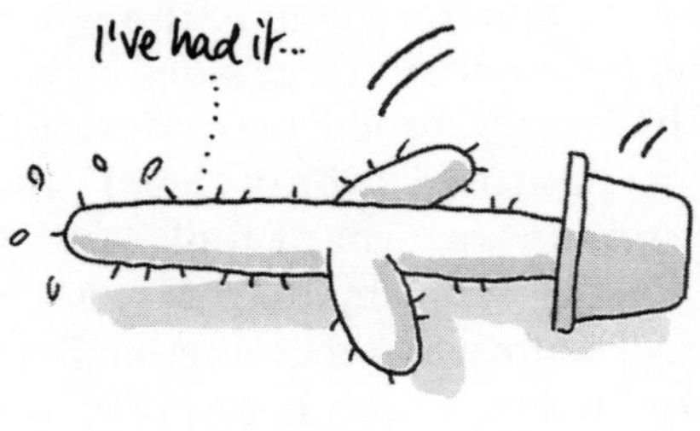

Notes

1 Or 'Bibles'. The terms are synonymous.

2 The repetiteur plays the piano score in rehearsals, fills in for any singer who is missing, coaches the cast and is generally indispensable.

3 Or 'British'.

4 Covers are very similar to understudies. However, they are not obliged to be constantly on hand. On the day of a performance a principal has to phone the theatre before 11.00 am if they feel they may not be able to go on. Up to midday, therefore, covers are standing by to whisk up to London or to the theatre. After midday their time is their own.

3
The Props Department

The Props Department lives down in Limehouse, East London, and I arrived there to interview Ivy Cannell, the Property Manager, after the *Xerxes* run – when her staff were deep in the construction of props for *Carmen* and *The Fairy Queen*. Alison Bray, one of the prop makers, showed me up to the workshop to wait for her.

It was a huge room, apparently airy (though all the fans were going full blast) and bounded on three sides by work benches. The centre was full of half-made props: two sides of fibreglass beef, a plywood coffin, a monstrous pink head and a couple of harpsichords. Around me was what I took to be the usual clutter of prop making: tins of varnish, hair dryers (for drying paint rather than hair), racks of metal tubes and hacksaws, some pots of paint labelled 'Carmen candy' and heaps of sawdust.

In a cubby hole at the back, Keith, another prop maker was filing down a fibreglass cast (of a human leg) which he said was for *Fairy Queen*. 'Actually, so is practically everything here,' he added.

I looked round the studio. A girl to my right was stapling brocade to a gilt chair that indeed looked very handsome and seventeenth century. Alison was at her bench working on a small grey rubbery creature and I wandered over to investigate.

She had a design of an indeterminate animal tacked up behind her, a pile of fun fur on the bench and a reference book, *Down on the Farm*, open on a page full of sheep. But what she was working on was clearly a rat.

'It's for *Fairy Queen*,' she said. 'There are going to be quite a few of them. They're powered by electro-magnets, and they'll all climb up the wall, and then at the right moment in the opera, they'll fall off on to their backs . . .'

What right moment in the opera? I thought but, on closer inspection, I had to admit he was a very nice rat, made of rubber and covered with little scored marks (to indicate his ratty fur). Actually, as Alison was going to attach fun fur to him, the score

marks were simply an artistic detail thrown in when she'd made the original polystyrene carving. She said she started off by drawing a couple of rats, waving her hand at the designs behind, 'But I'm no good in two dimensions, I just sketch something and go straight to three.'

'Did you do sculpting at college?'

'No, not particularly. It's something I discovered here. I'm going to give him bright red glass eyes, a pink rubber tail' (she wobbled a grey rubber one at me) 'and pink paws. I've splayed the front paws out a bit and made the outline quite sharp, so that they will show up well on the wall; you have to remember the people at the top of the theatre, they need a clear shape to see. Really, rats tuck their paws in under their bodies. But you can't worry too much about nature, people have got to see what a prop is.'

Looking round the studio, I said it seemed to me that people here did sculpting, upholstery, welding, carpentry – everything.

'Oh yes, we're supposed to be multi-skilled; but we all have our specialities. Anusjka over there is brilliant at upholstery. I can do carpentry if I have to, but what I like doing is sculpting. There's a dead sheep under the table . . .'

So there was; he seemed very peaceful.

'Also for *Fairy Queen*?' I said, sadly.

'Oh yes, and this dog.'

And she pulled out a life-size hound, very alert and shiny.

He, like the sheep, had been carved originally in polystyrene but had been finished by a covering of papier mâché, paint and varnish. This would make him tough enough for the manhandling he'd get on stage, though fibreglass would have made him even tougher. Alison showed me another fibreglass leg, taken from a cast of one of Rachel's (the apprentice) and was just about to explain the process when Rachel herself and a couple of guys appeared for coffee.

'Keith's done my leg again,' said Rachel cheerfully.

I asked Alison, as we went down to the kitchen, if the unfortunate apprentice was obliged to be on hand for any odd limb that may be needed but all I heard above the clatter was an ominous, 'There's the dead body of Hippolita still to make.'

Ivy Cannell turned up at almost the same time as the coffee and took me back up to her office. She told me she'd started as a prop apprentice at Sadler's Wells in 1969 and had been with the Company ever since. She still ran an apprenticeship scheme, 'Though everybody who comes here has had some experience, and they're all graduates. We are lucky at ENO, we can pick and choose, but obviously there are a lot of things that you can only learn on the job. Actually one of my former apprentices is now my boss.'

This was Mandy Burnett, the Prop Production Manager. Her early training in props can come in very handy when she is costing a new show. She can look at a set model[1] and form a fairly accurate idea as to how much the prop budget should be. However, a set model only tells you so much. 'They usually only show the major bits of furniture and the sculpture,' said Ivy, 'you don't get a complete picture of all the props. Mandy costs what she sees but it's not until I have the first meeting with the designer that I get a true idea of the show.'

I thought back to the afternoon I'd spent playing with the *Xerxes* model. It had seemed at the time to be particularly rich in props – tiny matchwood deck chairs and tiny plastic cactuses – but actually it had given no hint of the daggers, canes and hedge clippings to come. That sort of information apparently has to be extracted from the designer.

Ivy took down a production box and pulled out a tiny table with six beautifully turned legs, 'This is a table from the *Fairy Queen* model,' she said. 'The moment I see a model like this I start asking questions. What's going to go on it, to start with?'

Back in 1985 she had had the round coffee tables in *Xerxes* to consider: what went on *them* were tablecloths (easy), table lamps (tricky, but fortunately the Production Electrician had his workshop downstairs) and china for the Coffee House scene. 'We just went out and bought the *Xerxes* coffee cups. Now, this table (the *Fairy Queen* prop) has raised all sorts of problems. Look at these turned legs, for example. One of our carpenters used to be a turner so there's no problem there but I remembered having seen a tablecloth down on the prop list. So I said to the designer, is the table going to be covered? Because if it is, do we need to turn those legs?'

He had replied that it would be but the tablecloth would be drawn aside, like a curtain, so that you'd see all the characters' legs under the table and, as the table legs would also be visible, they'd have to be the proper seventeenth-century shape.

'Well, then I asked him if the table top was going to stay covered' (it *was*, so it could be made cheaply in plywood) 'and then whether he'd mind if the whole thing was made in sections. A table this big,' she held the little model up appraisingly, 'would come out at about 11 feet. I had already asked the Show Manager, and Bill Rafferty, (the Transport Manager) how they'd like the table made and they were very keen on having it in sections.'

I was interested to learn that she had considered the implications of the design for people who were going to have to stow the scenery.

'Oh yes, you have to keep an eye on size and wing space. That was very important with the *Xerxes* cactuses. David and I went through his cactus book very carefully when we were choosing them. We couldn't have one that would scale up to eight feet wide if it was supposed to disappear quickly round a five-foot corner.'

It became obvious that she had asked the same sort of questions (*viz*. What are you going to *do* with the prop on stage?) of all the *Xerxes* props. The cactuses were thought through particularly carefully.

David Fielding (the designer) came in with a collection of little cactus pots, and his cactus reference book, and he and Ivy had sat down to work them out. 'He said he wanted the cactuses carried in, one man per cactus, and that they should be large and set out in a grid pattern on the stage. I reckoned that, in that case, the largest cactus could be about 11 feet and, given the size of the stage, there should be about twelve of them.'

The next thing to decide was their weight and this, oddly enough, hinged on who was to carry them. Nicholas Hytner had initially given the job to the gentlemen's chorus. 'David said the whole point would be lost if the cactuses didn't look serious and real; well, if it had been actors, they're not singing, [so] you could expect them to pick the cactuses up as if they were heavy.'

The chorus, it was felt, might have their minds on their music, so they opted for having the cactuses light enough to carry but heavy enough to make it quite obvious that their porters were using some effort. They were given a metal core of two steel rods and carved in foam rubber with an electric carving knife. The whole cactus was then covered in fine muslin which, given its fine weave is extremely difficult to tear, and finished with a latex skin. Finally they were painted and provided with extras such as bristles and pith balls.

I exclaimed at their toughness and the cavalier way the crew threw them around. 'Yes, they are holding up very well. The muslin makes them very tough. Once you start making props you get to know just how the stage crew will pick them up. Anything that looks like a handle will be used like one – a knob of hair on a baroque statue, the arm of a cactus. Naturally they are used like that, everything has to be done in such a hurry. You learn automatically to strengthen those bits. Any statue with its elbow crooked will be flown from that elbow, it's obvious.'

I asked her how quickly the props had to be produced.

'Well, it's a principle of mine to have props ready for the singers by the time the rehearsals start. Obviously they've got to get used to them.'

To achieve this, Ivy has to take the model away and do a lot of thinking. What can she buy? Shows set in modern times are relatively easy to buy for but period shows are another matter; practically everything in them has to be made. The *Xerxes* deck chairs, china and extremely twentieth-century crowd control ropes were bought – the latter's red colour was entirely fortuitous, and everyone was delighted to find it zinging against the green floor cloth. Everything else had to be made. In fact there was so much to do that some of it 'went out', that is, given to freelance prop makers. Most designers have a list of people they like working with.

Having established what is to be made in house, Ivy starts to dish the work out and clearly tries to accommodate not only the skills but the preferences of her staff at the same time. One of the boys (Andrew Richardson), for example, had particularly wanted to produce the huge Mexican statue for *Carmen*; she showed me the indistinct photograph he was working from and I was startled to discover it didn't show the back of the statue at all,

'Oh, he'll have to invent that,' she said. 'I spend a lot of time telling them that they are craftsmen – interpretative rather than creative artists – but it's nice for them when they can invent.'

'But will the audience see the back?'

'Probably not, but it's cruel not to let a sculptor finish the back. The whole piece is conceived in the round.'

'Oh, so that's why the Handel statue has a back.'

'I should think so. That statue was done by an outside prop maker. There was so much to do for *Xerxes* it was rather a relief to send it out. It's actually a composite piece of work – the main figure was carved in polystyrene and the cherub and the lyre were stuck on separately.' (These considerations did not apply to the *base* of the Handel statue which not only lacked a back but was used by the crew as a handy storage space for small props.)

Once the work has been shared out, Ivy sets up a meeting between the prop maker and the designer where they will discuss the visual references, the materials and so on. Using this as a basis she can give the prop maker a deadline. She will suggest that the designer is called back in, say, three weeks and that the prop should be in such-and-such a state of readiness. Even if the prop is nearing completion it will not be totally finished before the designer returns, the prop maker will merely give it a basic finish and provide some colour samples for the designer to think about.

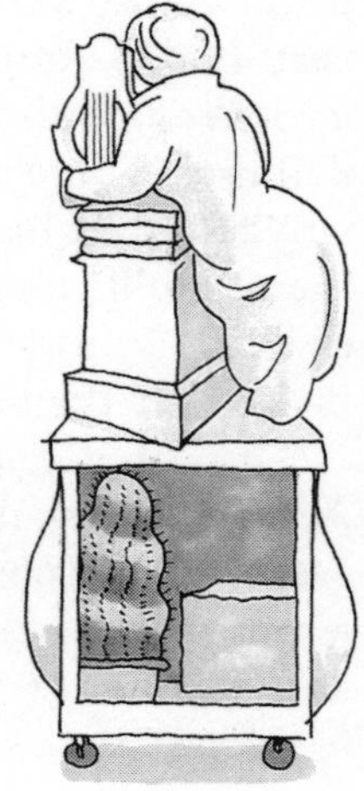

'The idea is to give the prop makers a run at it and then get the designer's comments.'

'And is it a two-way process?'

'Well, that all depends. Some designers get a real buzz when they see what we are doing and sometimes ideas carry across. The costume designer for *Fairy Queen* came in the other day to talk about the fox furs, and she saw the rats Alison was doing and immediately thought what fun it would be to have rat furs instead. David, however, is very precise. He knows exactly what he wants. He gave us an immense amount of references for *Xerxes* – Vauxhall Gardens, eighteenth-century prints of Persepolis – and he was always interested in our ideas but ultimately what he said, went.'

I went back a step. 'Do you usually do the furs?'

'No, that's Wardrobe but these particular ones had to be real little animals. There are some areas where we overlap. Jewellery, for example, is usually Wardrobe but we sometimes do decorations for costumes, they might want a non-practical[2] nosegay perhaps, or a bouquet. They usually do things like parasols,' (the material has to match the costume) 'but in *Xerxes* we did the umbrellas, or rather we dyed them grey. We bought in a batch of canes at the same time.'

I recalled some notes in a Running Wardrobe box asking for practice skirts, jewellery – and daggers. Didn't daggers come under Props?

'No, we don't have an armoury at ENO. Wardrobe have to produce the swords, and look after the ones we've got. In *Xerxes* they had to buy the knighting sword but I expect the generals' swords came from stock. Of course they just *wear* their swords but if there's going to be any actual fighting then the fight arranger will generally bring the swords in. He's the one that will look after them. He'll check for metal fatigue (rapiers are particularly prone to snap about four inches below the point) and balance; and he'll make sure they are the right period.'

The other department we curiously lack is a paint shop. The *Xerxes* backwall went out to be painted. The Production Department contract people in during the show to carry out running repairs on the paint work. The soft sets (the Hedge Drop and the Grass Carpet) also went out but the set builders are, fortunately, completely in-house. In fact, they share the

Limehouse warehouse. Their huge studio (it naturally has massive headroom to accommodate tall flats) is next door to the Prop workshop and they had just finished rebuilding *Xerxes*, for its loan to Antwerp, when I arrived. Having the carpenters on site can be very helpful, and Ivy was lucky enough to have the Production Electrician on hand as well. The lighting for the Egg and the Griffin were worked out on the spot. The Egg is deftly lit up on stage by one of the Wardens and it had to be cast, from a polystyrene mould, entirely in fibreglass to be translucent.

One prop that has come back to the house to be made is the Collapsing Bridge. It turns up in Act II as a model of the bridge over which Xerxes hopes to cross into Europe and is subsequently destroyed by Elviro and a thunderstorm. The Bridge itself was made in the workshop, with a tiny palm tree at one end – to represent the East – and a plane tree at the other, to represent Europe; this is quite invisible to the audience (see illustration 21). It sports two mechanisms, one to pull back the curtain with which it is draped (invented in-house) and one to make it collapse. The latter was made by an outside engineer, however, the Props Department are now into their third Bridge and can reproduce the mechanism themselves.' (See, however, the night of January 26.)

As we seemed to be running through the props, I asked Ivy about the non-practical cakes in the Coffee House Scene.

'Oh, David and I enjoyed ourselves there. We went through pages of cakes in a cookery book,' she waved her hand at the shelves of reference books behind her, 'and he said, "We must have a Black Forest gateau," and then we found a strawberry cheesecake. So we did those two. I thought at first that wood shavings would do for the chocolate shavings on the gateau but they turned out to be too brittle. We wanted to use an ordinary domestic icing piper for the cream and we eventually found a mixture of liquid plaster and glue that went through perfectly – and set rock hard.'

The busts of Xerxes' ancestors, smashed up in Act III, are made of fibreglass and indestructible. They are held together by an opaque glue – that does smash very satisfactorily – and are maintained by the Props Department in the theatre. That department also reproduce the lovers' letters in *Xerxes*, in fact, most stage letters are apparently written at the theatre. 'So many of the Production Department are ex-prop makers anyway.'

A stage letter should always say what its recipient reads out, although sometimes, of course, the letter is not read and the Production Department has to provide something it deems suitable. (Arsamenes' letter to Romilda in Act II is a case in point, illustration 10). There is usually some attempt to write it in an appropriate script and on feasibly correct paper although this depends on the show. I imagine the Prop Department had a hand in the beautifully made letter the Mikado writes to Ko Ko and had nothing to do with the various *Xerxes* letters that although written in a flowing hand, are photocopied for each night and scrunched up in the course of the show.

The last prop on the list, the Parterre, (see photo 'The Library Scene') inspired Ivy to do some space saving; its two bases did not need practical drawers, so she had them double up as huge show boxes. In fact, I saw Brian Kinsey (the Show Manager) methodically filling them up with props during Act III on the Last Night.

Ivy pulled down the *Xerxes* box for me to look through. It turned out to have samples of the crockery and cake knives used in the Coffee House, some plastic mouldings of the legs for the Knighting stool, and the wainscoting for the set walls. Like the Running Wardrobe office, however, there were all sorts of other boxes crammed on the shelves vying for my attention. The one marked 'Smoking accessories – pipes, pouches, snuff boxes and cut-throat razors' looked rather interesting but Ivy had moved on to talk about what happened to props after you had made them.

Rehearsals, of course, test them out, and create a demand for new ones. Amastris' tip to the Warden and Elviro's hip flask were demanded after the rehearsals had started. Most things have been adapted long before the Dress Rehearsal (which the Props Department consequently rather enjoys) but Ivy might go over to one of the stage rehearsals to see how the furniture is looking. She felt the *Fairy Queen* chair might need adjusting and we went over to look at it.

'Anusjka is wonderful at upholstery,' Ivy said as we watched her. 'She can strip and re-upholster a chair in twenty-four hours; that was a red *Macbeth* chair yesterday. I'll be looking at it when the show goes on stage to see if it works. If I feel the proportions are wrong, or the singer isn't comfortable, I'll alter it. I could make it higher, for example – though the proportions might go – but basically you've got to think of the singer.'

Thinking of singers, we paused by the two harpsichords I'd seen when I arrived. They were completely hollow and due ultimately to contain Richard Van Allan – as was the coffin. A washing machine, painted glossy black, was waiting to be gutted but I didn't like to ask if the unfortunate Mr Van Allen was going to be crammed into that as well.

As I left I looked across to see how the rat was getting on.

'Do you sometimes think the designers ask you to do impossible things?' I asked as Alison showed me where the electro-magnet was due to be stored.

'Well, kind of, but you see it's not our job to say no. You do what you can and try and make it work.'

It seemed to be the motto of the whole department.

Notes

1 A set model is a precise 3D model of the sets for a new production. It is usually made on a scale of 1:25 and constructed either by the designer or by a model maker. The ENO Drawing Office make technical drawings which they hand over to the carpenters (who go on to build the actual set).

2 A *practical* prop is the real thin; a *non-practical* prop is a fake. So, if an opera required the chorus to eat real apples they would be given practical apples – if, however, the apples were simply decorative, the Prop Department would provide non-practical apples.

4
The Cactus Run

December 16th

I returned to LBH after a gap of a couple of days and found the cactuses still set and Louise and Julia pacing the course for Xerxes' aria '*If you would worship the man who has spurn'd you.*'

The aria comes after Xerxes has shown Arsamenes' ardent letter to Romilda (which by now is wrongly assumed to have been written to Atalanta); Romilda is grief-stricken at her lover's apparent unfaithfulness but, to Xerxes' amazement, she still doesn't fall into his arms. He storms into an aria that swings between rage and impotence and, though his feelings are perfectly serious, the furious energy of the music might strike one as hovering on the edge of parody. At all events Nick Hytner seems to think so, and his staging of the piece has our hero frustrated not only by the inflexible Romilda but by twelve well-grown prickly cactuses.

In both 'A' and 'B' sections the principals gallop round the plants and their exact route was felt by everybody to be the basic starting point for this morning's rehearsal. After glancing at the Production Book I decided to try and illustrate the staging myself (see illustrations 4 & 5). The pictures show the cactuses, numbered and in position, with Xerxes' and Romilda's progress round the stage indicated by arrows. Significant Moments en route are marked by letters (see illustration 3).

Emma was called on to walk, or rather, *sprint* the part of Romilda and we immediately hit trouble as she and Louise bumped (A) into each other US at the start of the aria.

'What's Romilda doing wandering up there?' asked Louise.

Julia sighed as she looked at the Book which, good though it is on moves, is poor on motivation and Emma pulled out a packet of chewing gum with the air of one who knew we were in for a long haul.

Pending elucidation on this point from the real Romilda, we moved on and Emma hastily retreated from the King, dodging round cactus no. 9 to get downstage and reread the letter (B). By the middle section Louise had stamped down to the OP side and crossed over to kneel beside her and rip the letter away. The Production Book was quite specific about the stage picture here but rather lost itself in the next section, the *da capo*, in which Emma, unimpeded by the costume, appeared to be going for the Land Speed Record.

In the 'B' section, Romilda ran US again, retreated from the King (just managing not to sit (C) on the smallest prickliest cactus), dodged with him around cactus no. 8 (D) and made a dash for cactus no. 4, Capped 5 (E) and she was DS (F) for the last couple of bars of the aria.

The moves are of course timed so that Xerxes, who is chasing after her, does not sing as he runs but even so it is very energetic and by time they were circling cactus no. 8 Louise was not convinced they were reproducing the show. 'I think that's an optional run-round,' she said. 'I'm sure Yvonne wouldn't want to go so fast.'

'She doesn't have to, said Julia, 'her skirts give the panic.'

They worked on the gallop around cactus no. 5 again, but with less conviction. Romilda's final halt downstage at the end of the aria, and the King's reaction to her, clearly needed some subtext.

'I could try some rough stuff,' said Louise, 'but there was some reason why I knew I couldn't touch her. I'd never felt so helpless.'

Off they went again. However, as my diagram was now hopelessly entangled, I sat back to admire Emma's radical characterisation of the heroine. At five feet three inches, in jeans and fell boots, impassively chewing gum throughout Louise's tirades, she was unlike any Romilda I'd ever seen. Just as she loomed up on her in section 'B' the contrast seemed to strike Louise as well and she began to laugh. 'Yes, but I

never get anywhere *near* Yvonne!' she said, 'She's at least another six inches and then there's the wig and that huge full skirt . . .'

Everybody stopped for a tea break here and, while the crew jammed the unfortunate cactuses back on to the platform, Louise talked about Xerxes.

'I like him,' she said, 'at least he develops. Some mezzo characters are actually rather limiting. Olga and Dorabella, for example, you know they are going to stay the same for ever.'

I asked her what it was like playing a chap.

'Oh it's fine. I want to play more. Though there is a hateful side to Xerxes – there's his violence in the Cactus Scene. In fact, after that, I think he actually disintegrates – like the weather. By the end of the opera, though, he has accepted that he'll never have a normal relationship, he has to marry the official girl. I think Nick based it on Prince Charles.'

She said she was enjoying the acting and proved it immediately by swinging into the next scene (Xerxes' furious revelation to Atalanta that Arsamenes will never marry her) with alarming savagery. Nerys opted to be bewildered by this outburst and came DS for her aria, '*You advise me to forget him*'. She said, 'This aria is pain filled.'

'Yes,' said Julia, 'don't sing it out front – it's for yourself.'

As the *ritornello* started, Louise strode off US as though she was about to exit; however, as *opera seria* convention demands that she only exit after singing her *own* exit aria, it was not surprising to find that the Book indicated she should stop as Atalanta began to sing. Up to now, I had assumed that all Louise worried about at this moment was the pacing of her stride (so that she didn't find herself inadvertently in the wings before the aria started) but no, her subtext was much more subtle. 'I'm exasperated, I can't think what to do or where I'm going. I stop. I've never been at such a loss. Then I realise she's talking to me.'

She listened to the aria, bad-temperedly at first, but with an awakening sympathy for Atalanta that made the anguish in Xerxes' following aria, '*The heart that love has captured*' completely natural.

After this Amastris' attempted suicide and aria '*As you betray me,*' came almost as a relief. Paul promptly forestalled her and removed the dagger in such a hurry that he kept grabbing the blade. This drove Stage Management mad.

'Why does Elviro follow you on so fortuitously?' I asked Jean afterwards.

'Oh, we've been chatting in the wings,' she said, and for the rest of the morning she remained a cheerful antidote to subtext. I made some remark about the resourcefulness of Handelian heroines, particularly their habit of packing a disguise whenever they popped over to see the loved one on a surprise visit.

'Not me,' said Jean, 'I pinch mine. There's a General tied up somewhere in the wings – in his vest . . .'

The covers were on call that afternoon and, as they were apparently going to run the Act II scenes all over again, I went up to the first floor after lunch to see the people in the Making Wardrobe.

5
The Making Wardrobe

The first person I talked to when I got up there was Zeb Ibrahim, the Costume Supervisor.

A new opera production, from her point of view, begins with the first meeting between her, the designer and the costume budget.

'I find out what sort of materials he has in mind and then it's a question of getting out on the road to find samples. The range I bring back will include some very good fabrics and some that are just about okay. I can tell immediately if a material will fall in decent folds but we can't always afford the best. It's all about negotiation. As a basic rule of thumb, the more people there are on stage the less the audience will notice the quality, so we try to get the designers to cut corners on the crowd scenes. Young designers are very good about understanding about budgets and compromise but some of the older ones . . . (groan). There's one guy that knows everything. You can't show him slightly substandard stuff without him immediately spotting it and knowing where to get better; he even knew where we could get first class army khaki, for heaven's sake. We were only going to turn it into battle-stained uniforms.'

The samples she shows the designers are in a range of colours, some of which she will have dyed. 'A really intense colour has to be bought – Romilda's brilliant blue, for example; if you want the shot silk effect you have to buy it, it can't be dyed.'

Most of the materials will be natural, wool, cotton or pure silk, bought wholesale. 'They are absolutely the best, for dyeing, wear and hang, but the Company sometimes has to go for synthetic fabrics – even acrylic can take some dyeing. Modern shows, however, are often bought ready-made. '*Hansel and Gretel*, now that was all bought at Oxfam shops . . . that was great fun.'

As she started to talk about haggling and the rag trade itself her eyes sparkled, 'I've got a real bargain mentality,' she said, 'I just know how much things cost – I even try and knock Liberty's down.'

'We use Liberty's?!' I said.

'Well, actually, we very rarely get stuff retail. We use wholesalers and the drapers in Brick Lane and Berwick Street. You should go there, it's become real Theatreland.'

Once the material is bought it goes off to be cut, and the pieces are sent on to be made up by the girls and boys on the sewing machines. ENO employs two cutters, and eight sewing hands.

'The designers are very good usually at appreciating the work that goes on at this stage and the whole wardrobe loves making decent frocks[1] – especially when we are using good materials. Ten years ago people were getting quite depressed by the endless black and the trench coats. One decent show will lift you. We've just had an amazing time with *Kovanschina* – that had 500 costumes. This place (LBH) was very over-worked and excited – there were costumes all over the place.'

I asked if there was anything that made the costumes specifically theatrical.

'Well, we might have to distress them – to make them look grotty – and then there's the extras, you know, like blood or sweat. Or vomit, actually that's just cooked lentils and glue. The seams have to be quite large so the frock can be adapted, and the fastenings are very important A real eighteenth-century bodice would be done up with a real lace – the maid would have to pull it tight all the time she was fastening it. Theatrical laces are usually made of elastic so you can just lace the bodice quickly and give it a tug to tighten it at the top. Actually, laced bodices still get knotted up in quick changes. Dressers sometimes have to cut straight through them.'

Quick changes are naturally built into the costume though,

even so, the Wardrobe are rarely tempted to fasten things with velcro. It doesn't look right and sounds terrible when unfastened on stage – the old *Julius Caesar* handcuffs were a case in point. We always try to use hooks and eyes on historical costumes, partly because it is more authentic, and partly because they can't really go wrong. If a zip goes wrong all you can do is cut the singer out of their costume (and then sew them back in again) – you might not have time in a really quick change.'

'Thirty seconds is considered quite fast, two minutes, in Dressing circles, is all the time in the world. 'Dressers are brilliant, they can whip through a row of hooks and eyes as fast as you or I could use a zip.'

I asked how they kept the costumes fresh.

'We often line the costumes and the men wear sweat vests. The girls have sweat pads sown in at the arm pits, unless it's a tight look (the *Xerxes*' frocks are cut very tightly under the arms, aren't they?) and the linen is washed between shows. Of course make up on the collars is less of a problem now. Ten years ago we used thick pancake but the natural look is in vogue, and modern lighting is so much better that singers don't have to use much make-up anyway.'

'What about dry cleaning?'

'Well, it's not something we like. Quite apart from the expense, the chemicals get into the fibres and hurt them. At the end of a run the costumes are packed away as they are and not cleaned until they are pulled out again. You don't want them sitting there with tons of dry cleaning fluid eating up the fabric.' Oddly enough they aren't particularly niffy when you do pull them out. Perhaps it is something to do with the airy wickerwork baskets they are packed into.

I asked about making costumes for covers and immediately realised I'd opened up a can of worms.

'The problem is, we use up the whole budget – there's no money to spare – and I must say we sometimes take a chance on covers.'

The cover usually has a fitting at the same time as the principal to see if the costume will fit them or can be adapted. If, however, the cover turns out to be a very different shape, and the run is

you haven't made any cover costumes, have you?
VITAMIN C

fairly long (say, 20 performances), the Wardrobe will probably make a costume. Otherwise the Wardrobe rather hope the principal will stay fit.

'Of course we do two sets of costumes for two different casts. But on short runs we try and get away with one set of costumes. The only show that's caught us short that I can remember was *Lohengrin* last season. The girl singing Elsa was off sick, and her cover, was a completely different size.'

The crisis apparently blew up on the day of the show and the cover had to be dressed hastily from the Coliseum resources. As reproducing the actual costume was out of the question the Wardrobe had to improvise something at super-speed. They hacked up an existing costume in the dressing room and were still sewing her into it while the beginning of Act I was playing. Zeb clearly enjoyed the experience in retrospect – she said the dressing room was buzzing with adrenalin – and the singer (fortunately) took the whole thing in her stride.

'Tours, however, are another matter. The company can hardly take the whole Making Wardrobe on tour, so when the company took *Xerxes* to Russia they had to make all the cover costumes and buy the extra shoes.' (They were never used.)

'Once you've made the costumes,' I said, 'do you enjoy seeing your creations on stage? Are the Dress Rehearsals fun?'

Zeb pulled a face. Dress Rehearsals were a nightmare. You could never tell what people (producers, designers, singers, singers' spouses) would take exception to, and how much work any proposed alteration would make. She dreaded notes.[2]

'In the last *Tosca* Dress Rehearsal, they demanded we had to make a new jacket for a principal. This was on a Saturday, the First Night was Monday and you can imagine what fun it was trying to find anybody – freelance or whatever – free on a Saturday night.'

However, First Nights, I gathered, were a real buzz. The show is done, it's in budget, the problems are solved, there are no notes and mostly you feel that it all looks brilliant. And then there's the First Night party . . .

Just before the curtain goes up on the First Night the Wardrobe are on stage and in the wings making sure everything is okay and generally adding to the excitement. I quoted Georgie Perrott, of the Royal Opera House, who had remarked that some singers cope with stage fright by convincing themselves that something is wrong with their costume. Georgie takes the offending garment away, gives it a shake and returns it; did that sort of thing happen at the Coliseum? 'Oh Yeah' said Zeb, 'all the time.'

And, just like Georgie, she immediately sympathized with the singer. 'It's terrifying on that stage, of course they objectify their alarm. 'I can really understand that, there's 75 people on stage and singers suddenly feel they need attention – it's very comforting having somebody concentrating on you. You have to be so diplomatic.'

'Talking of diplomacy, do you have trouble fitting singers? Do you have to sell the costumes?'

'Well, we [the Wardrobe] all know the company by heart, you know, what they'll put up with and what sort of shape they are. Sometimes we have to convince a designer to have a sense of what will work on the people he has to dress. But nobody wants a singer to feel terrible. I'm not saying there aren't problems, but there's no tantrums or anything. I've known a couple of singers

take their costumes home to alter them . . . though actually if a singer doesn't like a costume, they just lose it. I've had to be with singers in their dressing rooms, and escort them to the stage to make sure they had all their costume on. Just for the First Night, of course, when the Designer was in.' (After that it's between the singer and any eagle-eyed member of the production team.) 'And then the men in *Traviata* hated their corsets' (intended to give them the authentic laced-in, pigeon-breasted look) 'and after the First Night none of them wore them. Of course, that meant that none of them could do up their waistcoat buttons for the rest of the run.'

However, most of the singers liked getting into costume.

'I think they like the weight of them, partly because it makes them conscious they've got a costume on – the costume is the part – and partly because they like something to push their diaphragm against.'

And the Wardrobe clearly do their best to accommodate their wishes.

'The men's chorus, now, they always want practical pockets and we put them in automatically, tucked inside jackets and shirts. I bet it's for beer money. Their dressing rooms are miles away from the canteen.'

In fact the only garment the Wardrobe seems unable to sell are hats.

'They all hate hats. They can't see from under the brim, the sound distorts and they know half of their face is in shadow. It's amazing how frequently they get lost. I sometimes think we ought to sew them on to the wigs.'

Once the show has gone to the Coliseum the costumes become the responsibility of the Running Wardrobe. They are handed over with a Costume Bible that contains photos of the costumes and a complete description of each one. And there the Making Wardrobe leaves them – until the re-makes begin.

Were they sorry to see them go?

'Actually, the worst thing about taking things over to the Coli is that so many of the Dressing Rooms are miles away from the stage and up all those stairs – you know how heavy the frocks are. I always think after I've got some up to Room 27, I—*must*—(pant)—give—up—(heave)—smoking . . .'

Notes

1 A generic term for *any* sort of costume.

2 Notes are comments on your work dished out by the director after most rehearsals.

6
Enter Nicholas Hytner

Nicholas Hytner arrived at LBH the week before Christmas to give the cast, or rather the newcomers, a day's rehearsal.

He started the session by running through the Concert Scene and immediately provided a much broader context for the subtext. As Xerxes prepared to address the Tree, for example, he said, 'Everything you do is public and for the public. You are very self-conscious. The Tree is dedicated to the greater glory of Persia,' and, as Elviro entered, 'You're a poor working-class guy having to cope with the romantic excesses of the aristocracy.'

In the Arsamenes/Xerxes dialogue that followed he even took us back to their early years.

'When you were Crown Prince . . .' he began. Louise looked rather startled.

'When I was Crown Prince . . .' she said cautiously.

'When your father was alive, Arsamenes was always pulling the girls. He was more successful than you, a Crown Prince has less licence. Now you think, "Well, I'm the king now. I can tell him what to do."' He added, 'I think that Xerxes has only recently ascended the throne and he's been throwing his weight about.'

Most interestingly of all, he was totally free of the Book. At the end of Xerxes' aria '*I will declare my passion*', Louise exited, giving Arsamenes the traditional slap on the back as she went. In performance the gesture can sometimes seem cheerfully irritating but it often appears merely awkward. Nicholas sat up. 'What do you do that for?' he said.

'It's in the Book' said Julia. (It must be ghastly to see one of your ideas carved in stone like that.)

'You can't do that,' said Nicholas.

'I've never thought it worked,' said Louise, and they all stared at Chris slumped in the DS PS deck chair.

'Couldn't I just push him?' she said, 'as he tries to get up.'

'Perfect,' said Nicholas. 'Push him back down. You're saying "Calm down – I'm going to have this one."'

She did so, with an insufferable grin, and the Book was duly revised.

All through the session he worked at making the action subtler. In the above scene, for example, he said as Louise and Chris began to spar, 'Don't crowd each other. The suspicion, and dismay, are implicit.'

And Paul got some classic direction on acting comedy, couched initially in a rather elliptical form. 'You know, Elviro would rather be reading Tennyson; he was born to write the definitive critical analysis of *In Memoriam*. Arsamenes thinks Elviro is Figaro, but he's nothing of the sort; he does everything he can to stop the opera. Of course it is a stock comic part, but you don't have to advertise the comedy role, don't energise. He doesn't want to be on stage.'

Even Atalanta's '*By stealing secret kisses*,' (which always seems to play itself) was sobered down.

'Atalanta never gets married, you know,' he said to Nerys. 'She always knows exactly how to run a relationship, but it never happens, she ultimately becomes a super-efficient secretary.' And then, moving in on how to play the aria, 'Try to see the audience as your best friend. You're having a cappuccino with them – all two and a half thousand – you're intimate, gossipy. If you are precise as to who you are talking to, it'll do itself. You don't need to demonstrate it. You can afford to be more dead-pan; cut out the soubrette.'

Louise entered for her first scene alone with Romilda.

'Toss off, "*Madam... your humble servant*"' said Nicholas. 'It's just like "Hi there!"'

And at the line 'Romilda, step forward . . .' he said, 'This is something Xerxes really thinks he can do. He's good at talking. Turn on her the full force of your personality, your beauty, your oratory.'

Louise turned right round on Romilda (Emma again) with a flourish. 'I've been playing it haughty,' she said.

'No, no, it's more volatile,' said Nicholas, adding apropos of the whole piece. 'It's very British. Everybody has a high level of embarrassment.'

He whizzed through all the Chris Robson and Jean Rigby scenes, cutting their arias as he went, and had reached the Investiture by the tea break. This was the first time I'd seen Mark Richardson (Ariodates) in rehearsal. He needed no direction on the gravity proper to a comic bass – although his meticulous attention to detail threw Nicholas for a moment. At the beginning of the scene he stalked solemnly on and saluted the (imaginary) Winged God with his fingers spreadeagled. Nicholas looked at him. 'Mark, why are you saluting like that?' he asked.

'Ah, that's my gloves,' said Mark, 'When I'm wearing them, they are so thick that they make my fingers spread out.'

Xerxes' veiled proposal (that he marry Ariodates' daughter, Romilda) generated a great deal of discussion; particularly as the misunderstanding here ultimately brings about the denouement. Nicholas said, 'Xerxes is barking mad, isn't he? If he'd just *told* Ariodates it was Romilda . . .'

'Isn't it political?' said Louise. 'Amastris is his official fiancée. He can't break it off just like that.'

'Yes,' said Nicholas, 'also he's testing the water. He's saying, "Listen, I'm going to marry your daughter but I can't tell you properly because I've got to square it with the protocol people. Are you reading me?" Then during the knighting ceremony he's smug, very pleased with himself, convinced that Ariodates understands what he's getting at. What he doesn't realise is that Ariodates is a fool and has jumped to the wrong conclusion.'

Mark immediately leapt to his character's defence. 'I don't see that Ariodates is a fool,' he said and – consciously assuming Ariodates' weighty air – added solemnly, 'It's the natural conclusion to come to, what else could I think?'

Nicholas paused for a moment and smoothly incorporated Mark's point of view into the subtext. 'There's something in that,' he admitted, 'Ariodates is rather a splendid person: weighty, reliable. He always comes across well on Persian TV.'

This was a new angle on the General, and Nicholas expanded on it for Mark's aria '*I never seek to question*.'

'I can imagine him in the Saloon Bar,' he said and (barking the next bit in officer tones) he added, '"In the British Army, y'know, we get to learn that things usually turn out all right. I mean this all goes to prove what I always say, good always comes round."'

Mark sung it on these lines, decent, self important and intensely serious; it was extremely funny.

It was in the Coffee House scene that Nicholas laid down the baseline for the entire production. Louise was trying to eat her chocolate cake again and had raised an eyebrow at Nerys' *da capo*. 'Don't overplay, "Oh no, another *da capo!*"' he said. 'It undermines the whole opera if you do.'

The session finished with Atalanta's subsequent aria and everybody went to lunch feeling that it had been an extremely stimulating rehearsal. However, there had been one bit of direction that seemed doomed to fail. As the Warden (Mike Afford) walked through the Hedge Clipping Scene, Nicholas had groaned, 'Can we play this as we did originally,' he said, 'as a throw-away gag? It's become a National Institution.'

It remained one.

7
Enter Romilda

LBH December 29th.

The first rehearsal after Christmas brought with it a new name on the Call Sheet. (See illustration 11)

Yvonne Kenny joined us after a run of performances of *Maria Stuarda* in Australia – and a dramatic recording session in Melbourne. Halfway through the recording of her album *Simple Gifts*, part of the studio roof had blown off in a freak storm, and left the recording company with a new studio (and sound equipment) to find over Christmas. They had succeeded, but the knock-on effect had played havoc with the *Xerxes* schedule and Yvonne arrived in England to find she was booked for an epic run-through of all the Romilda scenes the very next day.

Much later she recalled that first rehearsal.

'That was an abnormal situation,' she said, 'I had virtually sung the last note in Melbourne and then it was on to the plane and into rehearsal. I hadn't a chance to collect my thoughts. Of course I was under pressure to make up for lost time and I wanted to get the role in place for my colleagues. The trouble was that my brain took longer to reach England than the rest of me.'

Yvonne had played Romilda for ENO twice before and I watched, fascinated, as she rediscovered the part. Unlike Louise who, in a similar situation, had plunged immediately into the subtext, Yvonne reproduced the physical staging precisely.

I realised afterwards that she did this to access her previous performance. She had after all been through the process of creating the role; Romilda's motivation, and the stage action that

flowed from it, had been worked out two years ago but now, obliged to find the part at high speed, she simply concentrated on the action itself. As she did so the thoughts that accompanied it reappeared, apparently by magic.

Yvonne strolled on DS to look at the cactuses, her cheerful aside, 'That's a nice one . . .' tailing off as Louise approached. As she handed over Arsamenes' misdirected letter Louise remarked, 'Xerxes thinks this will do it. He believes everything that Atalanta has told him.'

But subtext was at a discount this morning. Yvonne was concentrating on the distance between Romilda and Xerxes and whether they were 'connecting', ie listening or looking at each other.

As she had read the letter Yvonne turned away to internalize, '*He deceives me, what torment!*' and let the hand holding the letter fall to her side. Louise tried to move in and found that, however near she got, she could establish no connection with Romilda at all (see photo 'The Cactus Aria'). The repeated phrases '*Will you love him?*' '*Evermore!*' rang all the changes from amazement and indignation to despair but, apart from a flash of disdain at '*What care you?*', Yvonne remained quite still, locked in grief. The letter dropped from her hand at '*'Tis the Fates that use me ill*' and her last '*Evermore!*' exasperated the King so much that Louise broke into the celebrated Xerxes stomp, upstage right, as Brenda (the repetiteur) played the *ritornello* for her aria.

And there we were at the very point which had baffled everyone in the last rehearsal, *viz*: why does the King start the aria upstage?

'Okay' said Louise. 'I'm so frustrated I stamp upstage, and then I think I'll have it out with her and I turn back. But then why's *she* upstage as well?'

To find out, Yvonne simply sprinted upstage left, meeting Louise on cue between cactuses nos. 11 and 12. They did it again and, this time, Yvonne remembered the reason for her action. 'Oh, of course,' she said. 'I thought to myself, "I've got to get out of here!" and I ran upstage in a panic, and then – "Oh God, there's the King!"'

Playing it again they discovered that Romilda was so unnerved by the King that she unwittingly started the chase and, after this, the 'A' section and the middle of the aria presented no problems – though the letter had a hard time of it . . .

Yvonne gave it a look. 'I've done everything I can with this.' she said.

As the *ritornello* played for the *da capo* she ran upstage, away from the king, bumping into him by cactus no. 9 and, retreating agitatedly backwards on to cactus no. 6, her eminently practical subtext came across clearly. 'I never know where it is? Is it here? Or here?' Prang!

Then off they went round cactus no. 6, upstage to cactus no. 8 – dodging each side of it until Yvonne made a break for cactus no. 4 – and a final anti-clockwise lap (around cactus no. 5) took them downstage, straight into the quiet close of the aria.

There Yvonne stood downstage between cactuses nos. 1 and 2 trying to remember her feelings the last time she played the part. 'I remember standing here like a tree trunk at the end,' she said, 'feeling very strong.'

They walked the 'B' section again, dodging cactuses, lapping the stage and coming to their abrupt halt at the end. And suddenly the subtext returned. 'Ah yes,' said Yvonne, 'I stop and *listen* to Xerxes and his line '*I should force you*' disgusts me.'

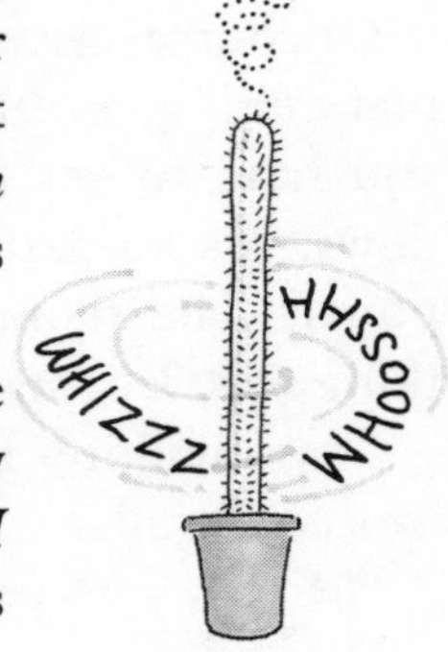

Louise immediately sang this line as she grabbed her arm. However, Yvonne turned away with revulsion, and Louise's last line '*But I cannot*' had to be sung in despair. She was delighted. 'Of course, that's why Xerxes can't touch her,' she said. 'Romilda has withdrawn from him. He suddenly realises you can't force a person to love you. If they won't, that's it, really, all he can do is leave. This has never happened to him before.'

Julia ended the morning session by taking Yvonne through the next aria, '*That ruthless tyrant*,' this turned out to be a simple matter of singing the 'A' section downstage OP, crossing to pick up the letter in the 'B' section, and exiting with it, PS, at the end. Julia paused to consider whether Romilda chucked it down again, but Yvonne was resolute. 'I take it *out*,' she said, 'I've done enough Letter Acting.'

I've done enough letter acting
pity, I was just getting interested

I asked Yvonne much later if she always rehearsed like this.

'Oh no,' she said, 'I'm not an acting-by-numbers person. There were two different people on stage that morning. I was *reproducing* my part, while Louise was *creating* hers. They're different processes. I was re-creating something I'd already done; I'd been through all the subtext before and the motivation was basically in place. It was my job to re-activate it.

Of course, once you've got it exactly as it was, the show fits into place and you can allow the passion and intensity to develop. But you have to get the geography right, from that everything else flows. It's so easy to lose a show in a revival, things lose their punch. The moment you *know* what you are doing, the whole thing lifts. But starting up is always a problem.'

I assumed it was even more difficult when you'd just dashed in from Australia.

'Oh, it's a very typical situation for a singer,' said Yvonne. 'You move rapidly from place to place and you are always having to re-orientate yourself, to reclaim your existence in the next place. Of course 24 hours later, when I had retrieved my brain from Melbourne, all the *Xerxes* motivation came flooding back. It was just rather hard work finding it that morning.'

8
Final Studio Rehearsal

January 3rd.

This turned out to be a run through of the entire opera – and a tremendously cheerful affair. Julia had apparently called everybody and by 10.30 Studio 1 was packed with the cast, the chorus, actors, actresses, Ivor Bolton (Conductor), Stephen Harris (Chorus Master), Nichola Bowie (Head of Movement), half a dozen stage crew from the Coliseum and some extra props that Lawrence had unearthed over the weekend. The Plane Tree and the Statue had already been set and, once the stage crew had crammed themselves along the sides of the studio, the rehearsal opened with the Concert Scene.

Given the numbers involved, the session was run almost as if we were on stage. Jane and Amanda McCaffrey (the Assistant Stage Manager) stood on the OP and PS sides respectively to give people their cues and, in Jane's case, to call out what would be flying in and out had we been rehearsing with the actual set; Amanda also took over the PS props, including the three-week-old practical cake (which she sliced up rather thoughtfully).

Jane called the Beginners to the stage, added a supplementary call for Arsamenes, Elviro and Romilda (who make their entrances shortly after the first aria), threw in a 'Tabs out' (to warn everybody that the main curtain was going up), cued in the Wardens who were to set up the deckchairs, and moved upstage to check that Romilda's port tray was ready.[1] I began to see that there was as much activity in the wings as there was on stage.

Louise's opening remarks to the plane tree were cut short after her recitative; indeed most of the arias were cut this session, though Romilda was allowed her two concert numbers. Her '*Swift from the mountains*,' was accompanied by some genius whistling the recorder part and, in '*O hark all ye wounded*' her port (diluted Ribena) decanter was brought on for the first time; Romilda used the tray to get rid of her gloves.[2] Basically, however, Julia decided to whizz through Act I and we were in the middle of Act II before the lunch break.

She paused at Act II Scene 7, in which Elviro tells Arsamenes of Romilda's apparent treachery, anxious that it should not come across as a mere cog in the plot. 'The men know each other well,' she said, 'they care about each other. It's not just a master/servant relationship.'

Consequently Elviro reacted with sympathy to Arsamenes' outburst over Romilda's unfaithfulness and, when his master pointed savagely at his hip flask at the line '*Perhaps you jest*,' merely responded with a reproachful '*For shame, for shame*'. Elviro's hip flask, I noticed, was a personal prop; that is, the Wardrobe deliver it with his costume. Julia added interestingly, 'They're both depressives – they set one another off.'

Having got the detail right, she cut Chris's exit aria '*Once we would kiss and play*' down to its last *ritornello* – and that was only played so that the actors could strike the cactuses and dash through the wings to wheel on the Bridge. The Storm Scene, minus its arias, rain, and collapse of the Bridge was over in minutes but, as Jane warned us that the Pillars were flying in, the rehearsal paused in its breakneck career and the last scene of Act II was run in its entirety.

The Pillar Scene starts with a duet between Xerxes and Amastris which they sing as if unaware of each other's presence (Noel said the whole piece remains an aside). This morning, however, one could not help but be aware of the chorus ladies edging along the OP and PS walls during the duet, taking their umbrellas from Jane and Amanda and waiting to be cued on for their Umbrella entrance.

With them came Romilda, under guard, and Xerxes advanced with his gift of jewellery. As Louise opened the case there was a genuine 'Oh!' from Yvonne and both of them looked inside.

'Goodness, we've got new jewels!' said Louise.

'Aren't they pretty?' said Yvonne, 'I've obviously got the wrong brother,' and she snapped the case shut, 'Thanks! Let's go.'

Brenda restored order with the *ritornello* of Romilda's next aria, one that is not blessed with the most lucid of texts. The 'A' section, '*The heart that beats contented, Is prized beyond expression*', is an unexceptionable sentiment but it is difficult to see how Romilda expects it to make Xerxes back off, and the middle section, '*False love dies unlamented – it is not worth possession*', could refer either to Arsamenes (Romilda after all believes he is unfaithful) or, sung as a reproach, to Xerxes himself.

In the show Yvonne made the aria an expression of Romilda's constancy but here Julia suggested that the recitative at least be played as a moment of indecision: perhaps she really *has* got the wrong brother. Yvonne walked the scene and toyed with the necklace for a second then, putting it firmly back in its case, she looked straight at Louise as she articulated her subtext. 'This is disgusting! You think I'm going to be bought by jewels!?'

She is saved, of course, from the consequences of this imprudence by the timely intervention of Amastris. This morning Jean dashed forward armed only with a prop umbrella, terminally surprising the two guards who retreated hastily.

Xerxes' convenient exit at this point – to give Romilda the chance to dismiss the guards and save Amastris from prison – inspired no subtext at all, he is so clearly impelled by the plot. However, Amastris' and Romilda's feelings about each other were another matter.

Jean frowned at Yvonne from under the brim of her hat as she explained why she'd rushed in. '*I saw he'd use constraint to make you wed him*,' she said, adding with a certain lowering energy, '*And 'twas not alone on your account that this grieved me . . .*'

Julia teased out the subtext as she paced slowly off-stage. 'Your feelings are ambiguous, you've saved her from Xerxes, and she rescues you but she's still your rival.'

Jean turned to look warily at Romilda. 'I'm thinking, What's she got that I haven't?'

Yvonne returned the look, 'And I'm thinking, he's odd.'

The act ended with Romilda's '*The love cross'd by fortune*' which went with such a swing that several people, the heroine included, broke into a Baroque disco dance during the play out. 'That,' said Ivor, with marked satisfaction, 'is my favourite aria.'

The afternoon was given over to Act III. We didn't actually have the Egg, but a Warden took up position beside its notional position while Brenda played the *sinfonia* and the rest of the cast settled back into their deckchairs. Jane called out, 'The cloth is flying out to head height.'[3] (Everybody got behind their newspapers) 'Here comes the Egg,' she added as the Warden appeared to trundle that exhibit across the stage. Another Warden entered and dished out

Griffin programmes and as Jane said, 'The Griffin is entering now . . .' the cast stared reverently at the (imaginary) Griffin spot, while the Egg Warden moved upstage to plug his invisible prop into an imaginary electric socket on the OP.

Meanwhile the lovers were pointedly *not* looking at Eggs, Griffins or each other. Romilda, Arsamenes and the unfortunate Elviro (caught between them) buried themselves completely in their copies of *The Inquirer*, surfacing only to glare across at the other's front page. Julia did not, however, linger on their subsequent quarrel but caught up with the action at Xerxes' aria '*I go in certain hope*', sung just after the king has bullied Romilda into accepting his hand. Romilda is pinned into her deck chair by Xerxes' two bodyguards at this point, and her attempts to move off are frustrated by their silent menaces. That afternoon they threatened her so nervously that Louise laughed.

'If it came to the point, *nothing* would happen,' she said, 'Romilda would eat them alive.'

All the Act III arias were in, including Arsamenes' 'A*h love, tyrannic love*' in which Chris pointed accusingly at the cartoon desk throughout, and before we knew it we were into the Quarrel Scene.

Romilda takes the timing of her slap from the conductor – (although on this occasion she gave Chris the merest tap, provoking Nicole and Emma to fondly recall all the times they'd stepped in for Romilda and got to slosh him properly). Both principals took the roof off for this number, stomping furiously round the OP wing between sections and blazing away at each other in the duet, while Noel provided the audience sound effects.

He has heard the audience's reactions a hundred times and wickedly imitated them – the premature applause at the end of the first section, a couple of outraged Sshh's and an amazed 'Oooh – Ah!' as the lovers rushed on again. In the last section Julia said, 'Play to the House,' although really they didn't seem to need any encouragement.

Shortly afterwards, of course, they were being congratulated by Ariodates on their engagement. Chris pulled at Mark's lapel as he said, '*Xerxes commands this?*' a gesture Mark obviously felt was too familiar. He disengaged Chris's hand saying, 'I know he's the King's brother, but I don't have to stand for this.'

As Ariodates joined their hands, Yvonne said thoughtfully, 'I clearly don't have a mother.'

'No,' said Mark firmly, 'She died years ago.'

After this came the Bust Scene ('*Rise Ye Furies*') in which Xerxes, furious at the loss of Romilda, smashes all the busts of his ancestors. (See photo Xerxes' last aria'). Lawrence set up the plinths, balanced the busts on top of them and Louise plunged into the *coloratura*. Each bust gets knocked down a different way and, while Louise was anxious to reproduce a remembered bit of business from Ann Murray – 'Anne always seems to just walk past the second one and push it petulantly' – Jane was anxious that she should really chuck them about, as they are absolutely indestructible.

This was quite difficult to believe today as Louise destroyed them *very* thoroughly. The last bust always seems to self-destruct by the force of the mezzo personality alone but I suspected Stage Management of having a hand in it. However, Jane was not giving away any secrets this afternoon.

In the last scene of all Louise got herself into a tangle with her sword. She normally just hands it over to Arsamenes by the hilt but today she insisted on presenting it resting on her left forearm. After a couple of goes – in which it tried to jab her in the tummy – she tried it the wrong way round and presented Arsamenes with the point.

'It's the right way to do it,' she protested, as Chris backed off yet again, 'I spent the weekend watching the video.'

'Cheat, Cheat!' chorused everybody.

Julia, quoting Nicholas Hytner, said that Amastris' revelation embarrasses, rather than devastates, Xerxes. He says the right thing ('*Ah yes, but I am unworthy of your forgiveness*') but with no conviction. As they staged the last grouping she added that Xerxes' distress in the final chorus is provoked by Romilda and Arsamenes' kiss: he is not just regretting Romilda, but a quality of love he will never experience.

Noel, myself and a sentimental Warden felt disposed to be rather melancholy at the Finale but the day actually ended with everybody checking out the stage calls for the following week and going off in a flurry of good spirits.

Notes

1 Romilda is offered refreshment halfway through the concert

2 The wearing of gloves in *Xerxes* has never been consistent. The King himself appears to put them on for official functions only, though he does so in '*I shall reveal my passion*' in a manner that irresistibly reminds one of a tap dance routine.

3 The 'cloth' was the Hedge Curtain which flies up to hover over the heads of the cast.

9
First Stage-and-Piano Rehearsal

On 5 January *Xerxes* moved over to the Coliseum for the Stage and Piano sessions and by 10 a.m. the set was already built, the lights focused and the Sound and Lighting Boxes (at the back of the Stalls) full of shadowy technicians. In the orchestra pit, the pit men had set a harpsichord for Noel, who was playing continuo, and a piano for Brenda, who was filling in for the rest of the orchestra. Julia and Emma had had a production desk rigged up for them over the back rows and some steps and hand rails built over each side of the pit to give them easy access to the stage.[1] Up on the stage the cast were about to work (at last) with the actual set, with all the props and as many costumes and wigs as were available.

By 10.15 the covers had arrived and settled themselves down in the first two rows of the Stalls but I was due backstage. Pushing open a heavy fire door, I walked straight into the semi darkness of the OP wing. It was a mass of activity and noise and I retreated hastily behind the *Fledermaus* scenery (stacked along the side wall), confident they wouldn't be needing anything from there this morning and, from the relative safety of the Act II banqueting table, drank in the OP.

It is extremely large, containing not only the scenery for other shows in the rep, the OP scenery and props for the current show, but also the Prompt Corner itself.[2] The Corner is represented by a large desk, set far downstage, from which the whole show is controlled: all the cues, all the calls, all the bells come from there. Of course, the Prompt Corner should be set over on the PS, the Prompt Side wing, but the Coliseum PS is so tiny that there is simply no room to accommodate the desk, so we have the anomaly of the Prompt Corner sited in the Opposite Prompt wing. In the trade, this is called having a Bastard Prompt.[3]

From among the flats for *Fledermaus*, the familiar LBH people appeared in a new and awe-inspiring light; Emma, plus headset,

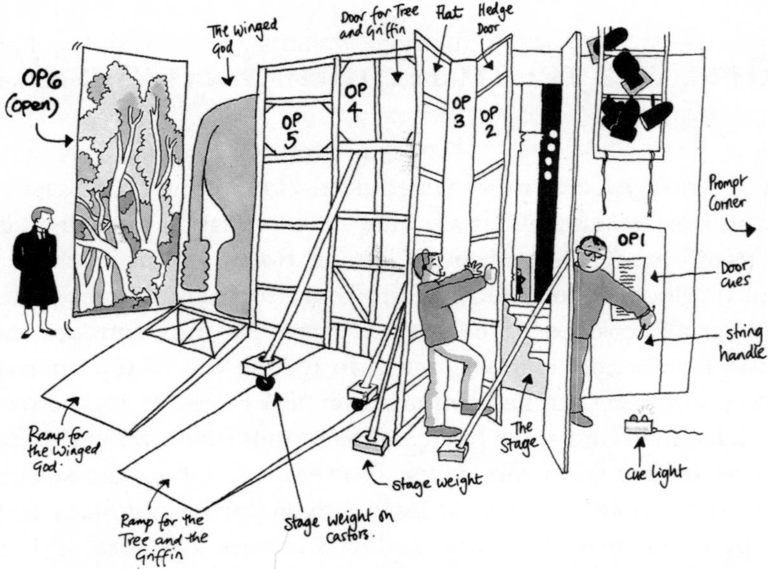

was clearly running between the auditorium and the stage, Nicole was fenced unassailably in behind the prompt desk, and Bob – also in a headset – was frowning magnificently as he tried to catch what Julia was saying from the production desk out in the Stalls.

As my eyes adjusted to the gloom, I realised with a pang that I wasn't going to see much of the show; it had never struck me before how completely boxed in the *Xerxes* set was. The back of the scenery, being invisible to the audience, was naturally unpainted and the bare plywood was carefully labelled (OP1, OP2, OP3, etc) so that the sets could be put together like a giant jigsaw.

Actually, though I did not realise it at the time, we were in exceptionally light conditions as the headers had not been set on the flats. This meant that the flats, minus their tops, were only three quarters their proper height and a good deal of light spilled into the wings from the thousand or so lamps up in the Flys. The sky cyclorama was set at the back of the scene but, as the weather effects were not used this morning, it picked up some beautiful shadows instead – sharp silhouettes of lighting bars and triple shadows of the Winged God, starting in purple-grey and fading to lilac.

In the wing the scenery was getting a last minute tweak – the stage crew were adjusting the stage weights and throwing up loops of rope to brace the top of the flats – while on stage people were stamping down the grass carpet, pushing on the Handel statue and walking about calmly through flying scenery and descending cloths. One guy shouted out 'Heads!' as the back wall came in and everybody looked up to make sure they weren't in the firing line.

Jane gathered six members of the crew round her and practised pushing the Winged God on and off. Like all movable properties, the God has a truck for its base – a wooden platform that runs on artfully concealed castors. Consequently most plywood props need only a couple of chaps to move them, and I was surprised the God called for six. However, it had to reach the built-up stage via a ramp, and doubtless needed the extra shove. This huge prop so dominates the upstage area of the wing that there is hardly any room to go round it. Most people learn to duck underneath. I noticed it had been built on the fine theatrical principle 'If the audience can't see it, don't build it' and conspicuously lacked a back.

Downstage the Egg was sitting disconsolately on a couple of *Fledermaus* chairs; it shares its display cabinet with the Tree and, as we were about to run the first act, found itself temporarily dispossessed.

Everybody seemed to be gossiping, those with headsets keeping up two sets of banter, one to their open channel and another to the people round them. Nicole, I discovered later, was capable of chatting to the Flys through one headset, and cracking a joke with Bob through another, talking to the idlers round the Prompt desk *and* giving a call out on the Tannoy system – all more or less at the same time.

Meanwhile the crew had discovered that I was trying to draw in the half-light and began to gather round to make helpful comments. Jim Johnstone told me that the headers weren't in because it would make the change-over[4] too long; getting them to sit flush with the cornices (which were also not set) took for ever – particularly as the flats were warped.

'The whole thing needs a re-fit',[5] he said. 'We only get away without one by putting loads of white paint all over the joins before each show.'

He smiled as he flipped through my sketch pad. 'What are you going to call the book?' he asked. '"It Isn't Easy"?'

By now the cast were drifting up to the stage, all more or less in costume and looking mysteriously six inches taller. There were no wigs or bald pates as yet which made for some startling reversals on the hair front.

Louise stood by the OP 1 door, trying out '*Under thy shade*' while Yvonne appeared upstage, by a TV trolley, to practise Romilda's entrance.

The monitors dotted about backstage mostly relay pictures of the conductor; some of them, positioned on the sides of the stage, are there for the singers to see the beat without spending the whole evening staring at the podium. Others, placed on trolleys in the wings, are for offstage

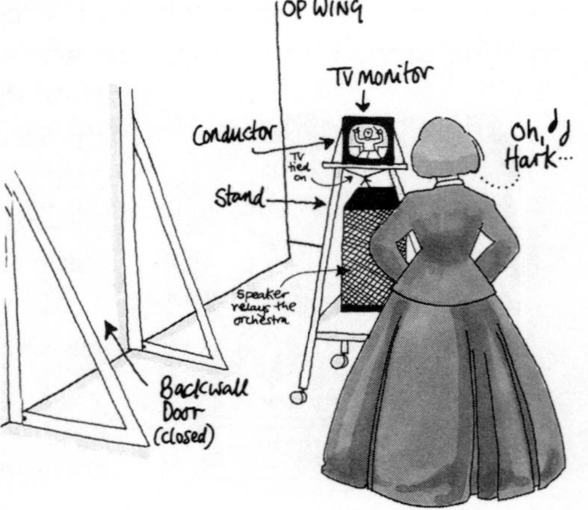

music and come complete with lighted music stand, speaker (through which you can hear the sound from the pit) and, in complicated moments, a member of the music staff to cue you in. *Xerxes* only has two offstage passages: the *sinfonia* at the beginning of Act I, and Romilda's first couple of notes, '*O hark*' before the Concert Scene.

The rehearsal started with an extraordinarily muffled '*Under thy shade*' from the stage, showing just how much sound a piece of plywood can cut out, and, though we all heard Romilda's offstage 'Oh hark' nicely, she disappeared through the double doors immediately afterwards and from then on Scene 1 became a series of smoothly pushed on props and carefully opened doors.

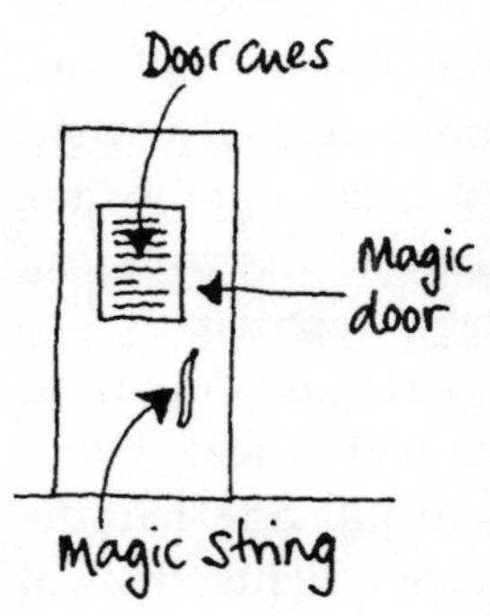

The most crucial doors from the audience's point of view are the magic ones which swing open the moment one of the characters even *thinks* of exiting; they turned out to be operated by a member of the stage crew pulling a string handle. The downstage Door 1 was operated this morning by Phil Kirkham. His door came complete with a sheet of door cues taped on the back, a magnetic hinge to ensure it stayed shut and a cue light to tell him when to Standby and Go.

A cue light comes on every time anything happens on stage whether it is a door opening, a piece of scenery flying in or a singer walking on to look at the cactuses; the lights look a little like traffic lights and they are placed by the stage entrances in the wings, up in the Flys, in the Sound Box, the Lighting Box and the Limes Box;[6] there is even one on the podium. The red light goes on just before the cue – this is the warning light, the *standby* – and the green light is added for the *go*, on the cue itself.

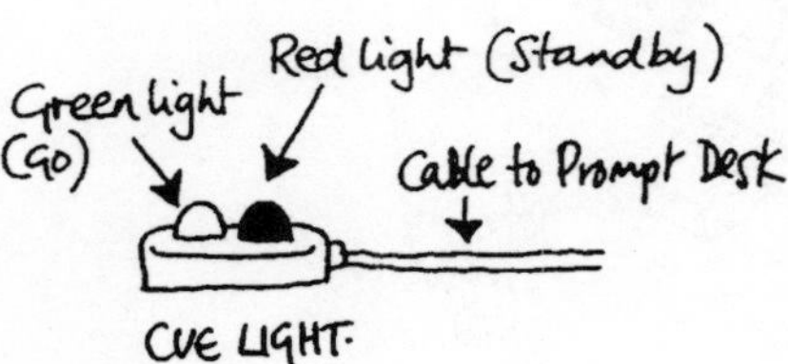

All the cue lights are operated from the prompt desk and, if the timing is very tight (or the Stage Manager has misgivings about a performer's powers of concentration) they may be supplemented by an Assistant Stage Manager standing beside the light, saying pointedly, 'Standby' and 'Go', as the case may be. This is called a Verbal cue. The Cactus Scene always got a verbal 'Go' as all ten actors had to start off at the same moment.

Phil's cue sheet listed his cues, told him whether he was to open or shut the door and how many people he was to expect to come through before he closed it. Although I noticed that the Wardens always came through saying anxiously, 'There's another chap behind, Phil.'

Ten minutes into the show Phil's cue light began to flicker and the green died just when it should have given him a Go. Fortunately the Warden who was due to enter (with Xerxes' gloves and cane) was standing there impassively and Phil let him on. However, he could hardly be expected to know, precisely, when people wanted to come off and Bob, who'd hastily grabbed a score, tried to give him the cues from that. While he was wrestling with the pages, Nicole sent out a call for a stage electrician.

Two minutes later another cue light went (a red, this time) on the back wall and Nicole, calculating that she had at least half a minute between cues, decided to check them all. She left the prompt desk at super-speed, leapt over the stage weights, ducked under the Winged God, ran around the back wall and raced back

to her desk in something under 25 seconds – talking to Electrics (LX) over her headset throughout.

Two LX guys appeared.

'Blimey,' said Phil, 'How many of you does it take to change a light bulb?'

'Only one,' said bloke 1, looking rather meaningfully at bloke 2.

Hot on the tail of the LX technicians came a member of the prop staff, to set Xerxes' knighting sword on the prop trolley. (See illustrations 12 & 14 for some prop plans.)

The prop staff spend much of their time bringing props to the stage, removing them and generally making sure they are all accounted for. There is usually one of them in the wings to relieve a character of a prop as they come off. In fact, a frequent cry from an exiting singer is 'Who do I give this to?' as they flap, shall we say, a letter. (This came as a bit of a surprise the first time I heard it. I'd just heard the singer in question promise faithfully to deliver the letter personally to the king.)

By this time I'd discovered that the base of the Winged God was one of the most comfortable places to sit on in the OP and I sat there, transfixed at the sight of Phil calmly reading a newspaper by his door. Paul, waiting to go on for the Hedge Scene, joined me. He said how pleased he was they were on stage at last.

'Everything is so approximate at LBH. You might have a taped mark for a doorway but, actually, going through a real door feels completely different. And things take longer to happen on stage. Look how big the area is. The size of the auditorium is quite a shock when you've got used to having the production desk two feet away.'

One of the covers told me later that he had some trouble adjusting to the size of the Coliseum stage.

'You don't realise how wide it is,' he said, 'and, if you are new, you want to huddle with the others in the middle and then, when some idiot moves off to the side, you feel like shouting, "Hey, come back! We've all got to stick together!" The wings are *miles* a away. They might as well be in a different country.'

The Wardens started pouring through the DS door and I moved

off to the side myself. One of the differences for the Wardens between LBH and the theatre must be the dim light and the obstacle course in the OP wing. In the present instance they exited impassively from downstage, scrambled over the ramps, whooped as the God loomed up and hastily re-assembled their features as they entered decorously upstage to set the ropes for the Investiture. One of them had staggered over a particularly well concealed ramp and Bob instantly called for somebody to gaffer it.

A chap behind me was looking for the 'treads' and although Brian Kinsey – who had kindly put himself on as interpreter – told me that treads were the stage name for steps, I had begun to feel I had taken on board enough technicalities for one day. However, I did want to know what on earth gaffer tape was – people were always calling for it. Jim produced a roll of evil-looking tape from his pocket and said that gaffering was almost any sort of tape, used in almost any sort of emergency. And, lo, during the middle section of '*When I see her*', when Louise scratched her finger on a rough edge of the Knighting Stool, there was an immediate cry for gaffering tape. Jim rushed forward – but it turned out the tape was for the stool rather than Louise (who was treated from the Stage Management First Aid Box).

'Don't worry, Miss Winter,' said Bob cheerfully, as he wielded a plaster, 'we've got the paramedics standing by at the stage door.'

The rehearsal ended shortly after this and the stage emptied in an instant. The singers simply melted away and the crew, conscious they had to strike *Xerxes* and set *Fledermaus* that afternoon, dashed off to lunch.

Notes

1 This construction is usually called a run-out.

2 The Prompt is usually the Deputy Stage Manager who (in spite of the name) is not primarily responsible for prompting forgetful performers; that job usually falls to the Music Prompt. The Music Prompt has a perch in the orchestra pit, so arranged that his top half is visible to the stage while the rest is hidden from the audience by a piece of scenery.

3 Logical readers might wonder why the wings are not simply renamed. The reason is that it is the invariable custom in England to have the PS on stage left and the OP on stage right; indeed PS and OP are practically synonymous for left and right and are extremely useful for giving directions. It is generally felt that the confusion that would result if the Coliseum were the only exception to the general rule would not worth be living with.

4 A 'change-over' is the change from one show to another; it usually involves taking down one set and building another and is (on the whole) a daily occurrence at the Coliseum as we swap between the morning stage rehearsal and the evening performance.

5 It got one, the whole set was rebuilt in July 1995.

6 The Limes Box is right at the back of the balcony and houses the spot lights.

10
The Prompt Corner

January 6th, Stage and Piano

I spent most of this rehearsal sitting behind Nicole in the furthest reach of the Prompt Corner, in fact my chair was technically blocking the first downstage entrance. However, as it is never used in *Xerxes*, I shoved aside a black drape and settled down to see what 'being on the Book' entailed.[1]

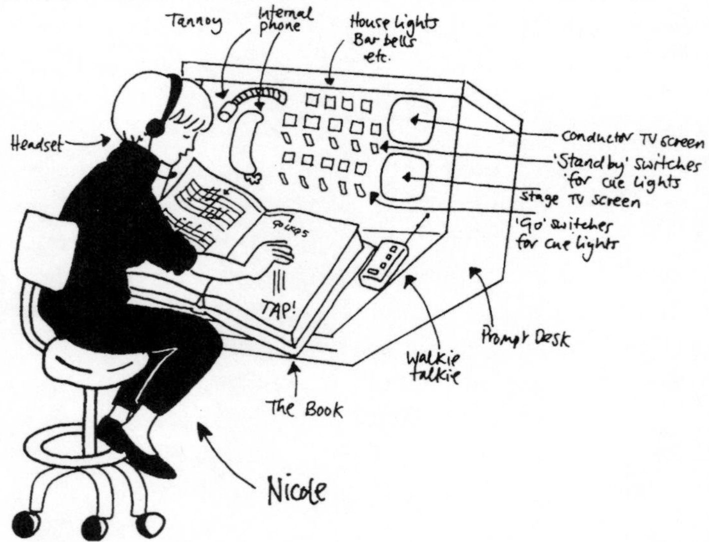

The first requisite for the job seemed to be to have no nervous system. Nicole was responsible for all the lighting, flying, set changing, sound and prop cues. She called the singers to the stage, brought in the tabs, told the conductor when he could start (but see page 118), set off the orchestra bells, joked with the Flys and dealt with emergencies. It was to the prompt desk, for example, that Jean Rigby was put through this morning to say that her train had been held up and that she was even now speeding to the theatre from Euston station.

The Investiture was imminent and Emma was summoned from the production desk to walk the part of Amastris. As she vanished into the PS wing, I looked over Nicole's shoulder to follow the cues (see illustrations 6 & 7). All the cues you notice occur on a bar of music. Miss that bar and you are in deep trouble. Nicole's sense of time was, in consequence, extremely acute. 'Can I see your cartoons?' she said between a couple of cues, 'I've got 25 seconds.'

Like the rest of stage management she could read a score easily although Brian told me later that everybody backstage was prompted subconsciously by the music. 'Most of us can do *Xerxes* blindfold,' he said, 'I just have to hear the music for '*When I see her*' to start thinking, "I'd better get the stairs clear for the hedge clipping."'

However, in spite of all this professional accuracy, I still found Yvonne's splendid unconcern, as she exited under the descending hedge curtain, completely unnerving, especially as I could see that Nicole was directing operations from a tiny, dusty monitor. 'Bring in the Hedge,' she called to the Flys, and then, to pace them, 'six, five, faster! four, three . . . slower . . . two . . . one . . . perfect!' and, to me, 'I must get that screen cleaned.'

She added afterwards that if a drop looks as though it *might* flatten a singer, the Flys stick some coloured Sellotape across their TV screen and stop[2] the cloth as soon as its bottom edge hits the tape.

As Nicole switched on the red lights for the magic doors she said it was quite a problem knowing how much time to allow for a standby. 'I guess the human eye can only bear to look at a little red light for so long, so you musn't put them on too early or the door operator will drift off – and then he won't spot the green.'

Even as she said it, the bloke on one of the doors went into a daze and closed it too early, leaving Bob Smith (one of the Wardens) on stage. Bob wandered disconsolately up to the door and knocked. The operator opened the door an inch, 'Yes . . . ?' he said suspiciously.

After that the Wardens came offstage giving the countdown with rather marked emphasis, 'There's two to go.'

'One still there . . .'

'Okay, okay' said the operator testily, and promptly shut the door on Arsamenes.

During the change-over from Act I to Act II, the Sound Department tried out their thunderclap. It came as a total surprise (I thought the Flys were falling down). However, the production team, who had come up on stage to hear it, seemed perfectly satisfied and clomped off back to the Stalls together.

The mechanics of the show suddenly became extremely important and as we reached the Storm Scene I could see Nicole not only had to call the singers but alert the Flys, the LX and the Sound Department to produce the weather, and the crew to be ready to strike the Bridge. She also activated the Superstar Strobe Mark II lightning bolt from the prompt desk (the Electrics technician was in the wing to make sure the lamp was placed correctly). The SM running plot gives a graphic description of the activity on stage (illustration 15) and in the wings but the busiest person is Nicole (illustrations 8 and 9).

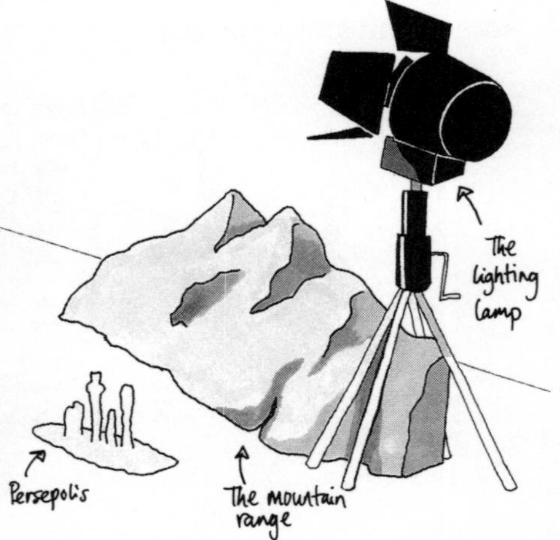

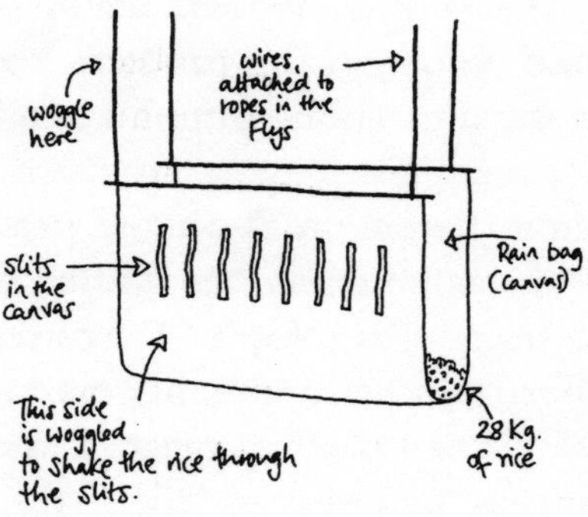

The weather slides were still not being used and the thunder, when it crashed in the Storm Scene, burst from a clear sky, as did the lightning flash and the rain. This was the first time we'd had the rain and everybody stopped to watch twenty-two kilograms of rice pour down from a snow bag. 'It's an old music hall trick,' said Louise.

Brian endorsed this and showed me how it was done.

The extraordinary thing was that it looked and sounded like real rain (even from a couple of feet away). Unfortunately, though it only fell upstage on Persepolis, the rice got everywhere and the distinctive sound in the wings, from the Storm Scene onwards, was the noise of rice crunching under foot. I asked Nicole if they re-cycled it. 'Oh no,' she said, 'We might sweep up nuts and bolts and things. It would be terribly dangerous.'

The destruction of the Bridge by a clap of thunder is always a problem and today, alas, the lightning flash went off before the Bridge had even been wheeled on.

Towards the end of Act II Jean Rigby dashed into the OP, struggling into her uniform coat, straight from Euston. 'Hi there!' she said as she ran past the prompt corner. 'I can't stop. I've got to go and save Yvonne.'

Her sudden appearance on stage caused a mild sensation. 'I'm glad you got here,' said Yvonne, who'd clearly had some misgivings about Emma's knight errantry.

After the tea break Nicole gave the call for the Act III Beginners. 'Your call, please, Act III Beginners, Miss Kenny, Miss Jones, Mr Robson, Mr Napier-Burrowes, ladies and gentlemen of the chorus, ladies and gentlemen actors.'

The call is given twice. I asked her how she knew whether the singers had responded; that, she said, was the SM or ASM's department. If the singer didn't appear they would ask her to put another call out (one begins to see why they are all wired up with headsets) and if the singer still didn't turn up, one of them would run round to the dressing room to see what had happened. The singers are called about five minutes before their entrance and the main dressing rooms are a minute away from the stage.

Sometimes a singer strikes a deal with the ASM, Jean told me that she did not want to hang around for five minutes in the PS, brooding on the daunting '*Vengeance on him who spurns me*'. 'So I told Amanda she'd have to trust me and I'd turn up just at the end of Chris's aria'. Apparently Amanda took this with her customary aplomb.

The rehearsal ended with the Quarrel Duet, and if the Wardens had had difficulty negotiating the OP wing, it was nothing to the problems faced by Romilda and Arsamenes. After the 'A' section they make a false exit US, dash down the OP and re-enter through the furthest DS door for the middle section. However, this morning they found they had unwittingly entered a hurdles race and, though they ducked under the God, swerved round the Griffin and leapt over a couple of ramps, they still arrived on stage a couple of bars too late – singing something that didn't sound like the text . . .

Bob started to highlight the ramps with white gaffering tape but Jane, who had rushed round to examine the route, sent him off for an arc light. Somebody pushed the Griffin back and the

'Ombra mai fu' – Xerxes and Warden. (*Bill Rafferty*)

Enter the King – Xerxes; note the small town of Persepolis at her feet. (*Bill Rafferty*)

The Investiture – Ariodates (*extreme left*), Generals (*seated*), General (*being knighted*), Warden and Xerxes. (*Bill Rafferty*)

The Library Scene – Romilda and Atalanta; the Parterre is the prop that looks like a large chest of drawers on the right. (*Bill Rafferty*)

The Coffee Shop Scene – Elviro disguised as a flower-seller and Amastris disguised as a soldier. (*Bill Rafferty*)

Amastris conceals herself from Xerxes. (*Bill Rafferty*)

Xerxes offers Romilda a necklace. (*Bill Rafferty*)

Arsamenes snaps. (*Susan Adler*)

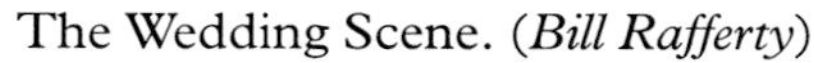

The Wedding Scene. (*Bill Rafferty*)

The Cactus Scene. (*Bill Rafferty*)

The Cactus Aria, 'If you'd worship . . .' (B section). (*Susan Adler*)

The Newspaper Scene. (*Bill Rafferty*)

Romilda is menaced. (*Bill Rafferty*)

Xerxes' last aria, 'Rise Ye Furies . . .' (the da capo). (*Susan Adler*)

Curtain Call at the Bolshoi Theatre. (*Susan Adler*)

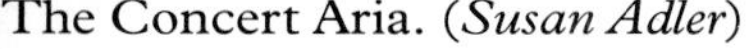

The Concert Aria. (*Susan Adler*)

Bald cap of the week; Bob Smith in the make-up room. (*Susan Adler*)

The off-stage band – The band are playing behind the back wall of the set. Note the long stem of the theorbo on the left, the costumed players (ready to go on stage with Romilda) and the Persepolis model at their feet. (*Susan Adler*)

The stage seen from the US in the PS Wing. (*Susan Adler*)

Final Call at the Bolshoi Theatre. (*Susan Adler*)

second run through was much less exciting, in fact Chris covered the whole course without taking his hands out of his pockets.

Notes

1 By the time we got to the stage, the Stage Manager's Book had become simply 'The Book' and the DSM (Deputy Stage Manager) who cued from it was therefore said to be 'on the Book'.

2 Actually they 'dead' it. Backstage jargon is completely death-haunted; an electrician, for example, is never ask to turn off a light, he is told to 'Kill that lamp'.

11
Stage and Orchestra

January 10th

This was a huge rehearsal that sprawled from 2.30 p.m. to 9.30 p.m. The whole set was in, headers, cornices and all, blacking out the wings so effectively that the door operators had to use pencil torches, to follow their door cues. I went off in search of a TV trolley to light my sketch pad. The OP was more crowded than ever; the chorus were in and kept appearing and disappearing from behind the folds of immense black drapes that had been hung along the length of the wing. Lucy Paget, one of the sound engineers, told me that the clean look of the *Xerxes* set would be ruined by a seam of light shining through a crack in the scenery and (as the audience tend to notice a light spill rather than a black gap) drapes are hung round the bits of the set that have buckled.

The orchestra were already in the pit tuning up (the mike on my TV trolley was obviously set right next to the bassoon) and Ivor climbed up on to the podium to direct the rehearsal. Once the orchestra are in, the control shifts from the producer to the conductor and, although the production desk was still in evidence this afternoon, it was Ivor who now called the shots and decided on the order of scenes. He elected to go straight through the opera, cutting the odd aria (usually one of Chris Robson's) and, in the ten or fifteen minutes thus saved, he ran through any music he wasn't happy with, in a block, at the end of each act.

In charge at last!
TV trolley

The OP swung into its usual routine: the singers came as they were called and disappeared on to the stage; the Wardens ran in to collect programmes and knighting swords, and the technicians opened doors and steadied the Winged God as it ran up its slope, however, a sudden flurry of activity in the PS wing, during the aria, '*When I see her*', came as a complete surprise until I realised with a thrill that I was about to see the Hedge Clipping Scene, from the other side of the Hedge Curtain.

Mike Afford, the Warden who trims the top of the hedge, was already stationed on his ladder and, as soon as the bottom of the Hedge had hit the stage, he was pushed on by two technicians – looking for all the world like a Roman in his chariot – while Amanda dashed in front, flinging deck chairs out of his path (the noise is covered, in performance, by the sound of applause). Meanwhile the Winged God, in the few seconds during which the stage was completely covered by the Hedge, was rapidly rolled back through its upstage door and, by the time the top of the curtain was visible, the God had gone and Mike was in position, complete with impassive face and shears.

Even so there still seemed an awful lot of people below him. Jim and John were clearly there to steady the trolley while Bob, half way up the steps, flung the clippings (bits of green carpet) over the top and kept a wary eye on the level of the curtain. Jane and Amanda hovered below, consulting their Running Plots and looking mildly anxious. I asked Amanda, later, if Mike was cued, 'Oh no, he does the whole thing in his own time. Obviously he's got to react to Paul and Chris. Jane and I are waiting for the next scene change.'

I looked at Jane's Running Plot afterwards and discovered that the two minutes before Mike's appearance must be her busiest in the show. (Illustration 15)

The phrase 'hedge dead' in this list became clearer as

Brian reminisced about the times when the hedge had not come in dead on its mark.[1]

'Once it didn't come in far enough and we just had a pair of shears waving about at the top, but the worst was when it came in too low; the ASM with the clippings jumped off the steps very quickly, but the Warden just had to stand there. Everybody could see the top of stairs.'

As the Hedge Clipping Scene finished, a dead calm descended over the stage. In front of the curtain Chris sang his aria, '*When pain and grief assail me*' to the quietest of accompaniments, and it was impossible to move so much as a deck chair. People flopped down on chairs and stared thoughtfully up at the Flys waiting for the *ritornello* that heralds Amastris' '*Vengeance on him*'. As soon as it started (Jean sings it in front of the hedge curtain), the stage burst into activity and the Investiture was cleared away and the Library set before she had reached the 'B' section.

Half the principals were by now in wigs and I was just deciding to pay a visit to the Wig Room when I bumped into Nerys who had just finished the act with '*By stealing secret kisses*'. She was in a straightish wig and was beginning to think it was something of a mistake.

'Weren't you given the old one?' I asked.

'Oh no, I'm not Lesley's colouring. I've been offered four wigs, all slightly different colours, I suppose I'll just work through them.'

After the break I moved across to the PS wing and bumped straight into Amanda who was prising the practical cake out of its box. 'Hi!' she said. 'We were wondering when you were going to turn up over here. Trust you to pick the Cake Act.'

Act II, I discovered, was dominated by the practical cake (a chocolate gateau, bought fresh every night). The particular one she was decanting at this moment had already unfrozen and was blobbing about alarmingly as she was trying to get it on to a plate.

Looking around, I couldn't see where I could get out of the way.

The Cake with Stage fright

The wing's tiny area was already crammed with tables and chairs for the Coffee House Scene, the Parterre, the Handel statue, the ubiquitous cactuses and a large scaffold that supported the three projectors for the weather effects. Downstage, a loaded prop trolley was parked by the first downstage door and here Amanda hovered all evening, following her score (laid across the non-practical cakes) with a pencil torch while dishing out crockery, canes, and programmes by the aid of light spills from the stage. However, she suspended operations to whisk a couple of black drapes out of the way, unearth a music stand, get one of the LX chaps to light it up and there I was, set up just behind the prop trolley for the rest of the show.

Before the Act started, Amanda thrashed out the chain of command backstage. The Stage Manager (Jane) was responsible for the running of the show and had as many Assistant Stage Managers as the opera needed. In the case of *Xerxes* there were two: one to run the PS (Amanda) and one to help Jane over in the busy OP wing. (Bob). The Deputy Stage Manager (Nicole) was on the Book. At the Coliseum all the ASM's get a chance to be on the Book and even stage manage a show, although the shows vary greatly in difficulty. *Mikado* practically runs itself, while *Christmas Eve* was a nightmare.

The PS wing I found had its own atmosphere, it seemed to be in its own little time-warp.

'You're usually alone in the PS,' said Amanda, 'and you have to be telepathic. Stage rehearsals are all over the place. The producer or the conductor decide on which order to run the show – not necessarily in the correct one – and the Stage Manager makes it happen, you know, checking that the right techs are handy, getting the Egg out, that sort of thing. Of course, all that is happening in the OP. The PS is miles away from the nerve centre. You just have to rely on your headset.'

At this point Act II was upon us and the Coffee House Scene swung into action. The Wardens ran in and out for cups, cakes and trays, while Amanda kept an amazing mental tally of the various bits of crockery coming and going. She had no other ASM to help her and, possibly because of this, though I was more inclined to put it down to the cake, the atmosphere in the wing was very cheerful indeed.

As the cake approached its final exit, the vultures (the gentlemen of the chorus and the crew) began to gather and, the moment it was wheeled off downstage, they swooped. The chorus ladies, who exit away upstage, never had a chance.

'I have to refuse that cake on stage,' said one girl, looking sadly at the empty plate and although Yvonne (waiting to go on for the Cactus Scene) pointed out a few crumbs that had been overlooked, she didn't cheer up.

Further upstage, a new girl from Wardrobe had arrived, staggering under a pile of gardening aprons.

'Does anybody know this show?' she asked generally. 'They told me to wait here.'

Before she could finish, the Wardens descended on her, grabbed their aprons and were off, pulling on aprons and collecting cactuses as they went.

Returning downstage, I found Keziah Walmsley, with a couple of girls from Wigs, leaning against the prop trolley, watching the Wardens glumly. The Wigs Department at the Coliseum is, properly, the Wigs and Make up Department, and Keziah (and her colleagues) had been entrusted with the task of making sure that the Wardens stayed white.

'Is that difficult?' I asked.

She looked at me wearily.

'Difficult? Take your eyes off them for

a moment and they go pink. Look at that one over there, what do they *do* to themselves?'

I gathered the Make up department wasn't allowed to whiten the insides of their ears but otherwise the evil paste (she showed me a tin of it) was applied remorselessly. The principal nuisance was that, although the stuff comes off fatally easily when applied to the human neck, it stains black cloth FOR EVER and, at the end of the show, the coats are rushed to a spare dressing room for treatment.

'We spray the collars with dry cleaning fluid immediately and, well, you know how well ventilated those dressing rooms are. We're spaced out in half an hour.'

She said that the Wardens' bald pates can be fitted, by dint of long practice, in a quarter of an hour. In fact they send out people from Wigs when the show goes abroad, to show foreign opera houses how to do it.

'You should come round to the Wig Room and watch us,' she said.

'Better still,' she added, 'come and have it done yourself. There's nothing like experiencing it.'

The Wardens exited shortly after this and, leaving the Make up department to move in, I joined a group who were examining the cactuses. They had obviously had a tough rehearsal and Brian was

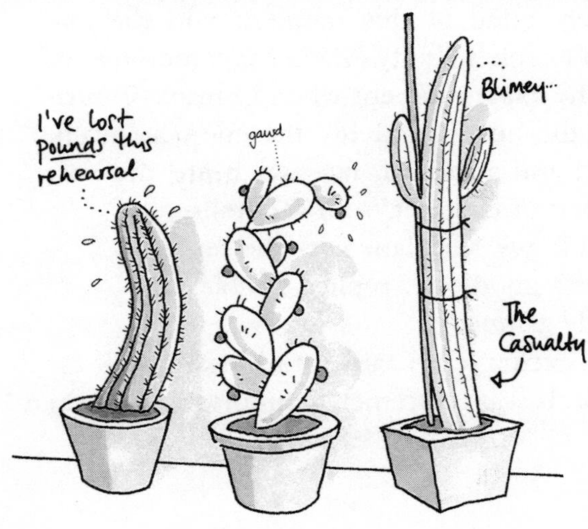

bracing up the tallest plant with a metal rod. It looked just like an outsize flower cane. 'The Winged God looks pretty shabby from the Stalls,' said somebody gloomily, and they all disappeared over to the OP to inspect it. I stayed behind to look at the busts, particularly the one that appears to self-destruct (with its plinth) on stage.

'How does that work?' I asked Amanda.

'It's magic,' she said. 'Actually, you ought to stay PS to see it.'

Thus encouraged I joined the semicircle round Jane as Xerxes launched into '*Rise Ye Furies*' at the close of Act III. She was kneeling by a tiny hole (bashed in the bottom of a PS flat) while she wound some fishing line round a reel of masking tape.

'Is that something technical?' I asked.

'Oh no,' she said, 'it protects my hand as I yank the line away. I just use the reel as a handle. The bust mechanism is very simple. The line goes inside the pillar and then, as I pull it, it releases a bolt.'

The last section of the aria began and she crouched down, intent on her headset. The PS side is completely blind at this moment and the cue depends on Nicole's ability (via her tiny monitor) to anticipate the exact moment when Louise will turn to glare at the bust. Suddenly the cue was given, Jane yanked and a second later we heard the bust fall, to a burst of laughter from the stalls.

'How did it go?' said Jane over the set,

'That was a good one,' replied Nicole.

Everybody grinned.

After this excitement I sank into Xerxes' chair for the last scene of the opera. It was extremely comfortable. I wished I'd found it before.

Notes

1 An object that is 'dead' or 'on its dead' is precisely placed. It might also be *obsolete* the context usually ensures that the meaning is quite clear.

12
Wigs and Make up

I visited the Wig Room after the run, just in time to see the *Xerxes* wigs being packed up for performances in Antwerp. Eddie Fergusson (Wig and Make up Technician) was dressing Rosina's wig for *Barber* when I arrived. It was made mostly of hair but, to my surprise, it had some golden synthetic threads woven into it. He explained that the wigs had to be re-dressed after every performance as the hair is woven on to a fine weave mesh and picks up sweat from the real hair underneath. 'Wigs act just like ordinary hair,' he said. 'If you got under all those lamps, and danced and' (here he waved his hand at Titania's wig) 'had tiaras put on and off, *you'd* need to re-do your hair.'

The Wig Department delivers and fits wigs before a show or a rehearsal, and collects them afterwards. They also help out with making up 'If we are needed. Many people like to take time over their own Make up, actually; they find it relaxing before a show.'

Eddie and his colleagues were a day ahead of themselves and the *Fairy Queen* wigs had already been reset (for the First Night the following day) while the *Barber* wigs were being re-dressed as we spoke. The room looked like a normal hairdressing salon – without the customers. All around us blocks of hair were being brushed, curled or, and this was a disconcerting sight, stacked in a heater to dry.

Of course not all operas require immaculate coiffures. The nieces' wigs in *Peter Grimes*, for example, had grease combed through them before every show, to make them look tacky, while the convict wigs for the old production of *From the House of the Dead* had great razor shaves slashed across them. Felicity Palmer's wig in *Mazeppa* was uniquely mistreated; she had to cut chunks out of it during the performance and, presumably, had a fresh one every night.

I asked Eddie about the hair they used.

'Well, it's mostly European and very expensive, £30 an ounce, but it is very good quality, finer and more versatile than other sorts of hair.[1] A lot of hair comes from Russia at the moment but oriental hair is cheaper – and coarser. We save money by mixing the types. Of course we have to dye the oriental hair. Unless we really need black, no European hair is really black, it's always got some red in it.'

He pulled open a drawer and showed me the swatches of hair inside, arranged in colour.

'Some sorts of hair are very expensive, real blonde, for example, or long strands of white hair. You see, a strand of hair has to be at least eight inches long for us to be able to handle it and knot it on to the mesh – even if it's going to end up as a crew cut – well, *very* few white-haired people grow their hair that long. Of course, we fake the length sometimes. Melisande's wig was faked. I mean *nobody* grows eight feet of hair.'

We paused to watch Lucy Smith (another of the eight Wig Technicians) knotting hair on a mesh.

'How long would it take you to make a wig?' I asked her.

'Oh, about three or four days.'

'And do you have to use natural hair?'

'Yes, nothing beats it, just for the look.'

'We use nylon if we think we can get away with it,' said Eddie, indicating the shiny silver wigs used by the *Fairy Queen* butlers, which were totally synthetic.

'And sometimes we make the front of real hair and weave in nylon at the back. The long hair worn by some of the men in *Fairy Queen* is half and half.'

Xerxes of course demands the famous bald pates.

'Of course, everybody uses them now but I bet we're still the fastest in fitting them.'

Speed is in fact something of a Wig Department speciality. Eddie has to go on in Act I of *Der Rosenkavalier* as the Hairdresser and I asked him how much time he really had to dress the Marschellin's hair,

'I look as if I'm working on the hair for ages,' he said, 'but really, I've only got about 15 seconds to put it up and *once* it's up there's no time to change it. Of course when you do hair down here, you keep standing back to see what it looks like but you can't do that in the show. So, though it won't fall down, it could easily look out of balance. After I've put it up the Italian Tenor has his big moment and I just fiddle about, because you can't upstage him. And then she says, 'Oh you've made me look old', but you can't do anything then.'

I watched his performance with new respect during the next *Rosenkavalier* and found I was standing next to one of his colleagues,

'I think this is the best scene in the opera,' she said.

Notes

1 Ron Freeman, the Wig Master of the Royal Opera House, swears by Italian hair, particularly if it comes from an Italian convent; it apparently has a wonderful silky texture.

13

Dress Rehearsal and First Night

12 January

At last the Company were to play in front of an audience and, as I entered the OP wing on the 12th, I heard an unaccustomed buzz of noise on the other side of the tab: the Friends of ENO were in to watch the Dress Rehearsal. There was a fair degree of excitement in the wing itself, singers hugged each other as they came up to the stage and made encouraging remarks, like Yvonne's '*Toi Toi Toi!*' directed to Louise down by the DS door.[1] Louise herself was muttering, 'It's ridiculous!' in protest against her own nerves.

The rehearsal started at 10.30, which meant that most of the cast would have been in the theatre from eight o'clock onwards, dressing, putting on their faces and, most importantly, warming up. Foreign singers, appalled at the prospect at singing top Fs first thing in the morning, would have one believe that the English custom of morning Dress Rehearsals is unique.[2] However, with another show due to come at night, the afternoons at the Coliseum have to be spent changing sets. As it was, the crew barely had time to build *The Two Widows* when the *Xerxes* rehearsal eventually finished at 1.30 p.m.

On stage, the crew and Stage Management team were deeply preoccupied: 'Eleven technicians. Just enough to run the show,' muttered somebody, while Jane, Brian and Bob watched the rice bag inching its way painfully up to the flies. It took five minutes to get there as it had to be raised inch by inch; one side needs to be higher than the other to stop the rice falling out. Meanwhile,

Hurry up!
I have first night nerves like everyone else...

DS, the Hedge Curtain had just lost a wire and was taking ages to come in and out.

An open Dress Rehearsal is run like a real show although the singers may sometimes mark their parts (that is, not sing out) if the First Night is very imminent. However, this morning everybody seemed pleased to have an opportunity to sing the opera right through. Chris Robson disappeared into the depths of the OP to have a final warm-up (it sounded very like '*Under thy shade*') and Ivor Bolton stood beside the prompt desk, waiting for an ASM to escort him down to the Pit.[3]

Everybody was in performance mode and the show took off immediately. The arias were delivered with such energy that people in the wings started beating time against the prop trolley and bits of the scenery, and Louise's furious (and unscripted) 'Out!' at the start of the Cactus Scene was so terrifying that the two actresses who caught the brunt of it came off still reacting.

Louise herself stamped past shortly afterwards, landed me a friendly buffet between the shoulder blades and, still clearly a Persian king, marched straight down to her dressing room. She said afterwards that she usually spent her time there, deep in the score, reading up the next scene. I noticed that the singers barely paused as they came off stage, even if followed by a burst of applause. Yvonne and Chris received an immense hand after the Quarrel Duet but they scarcely flickered as they swept off to their dressing rooms. 'Mind you,' said Chris afterwards, 'You'd notice if you didn't get applauded.'

Jean Rigby was particularly cheerful. I bumped into her as she was dashing off to pinch her disguise and found that not even the prospect of the dreaded '*Vengeance on him who spurns me*' could damp her spirits,

'I'll be glad to get that out of the way,' she said. 'I'm a bit tight about it, although it helps in a way, after all the aria is angry. But, once it's over I can enjoy the show. I love the cactus one' ('*As you betray me*').

She pointed out that, since only Ariodates wears a red uniform, Amastris must have pinched one of his spare coats.

'I imagine that his batman is being *very* evasive at the moment. He's probably saying the campaign trunk was re-routed via Athens.'

I did not see her again until the end of Act II, when she exits into the OP during the Pillar Scene; this morning she dashed into the wing, tore off her gloves . . . and put them on again. 'Phew, what a relief,' she said (preparing to run on again to save Romilda) 'I'd got them on the wrong hands.'

Dressers, gloves and other personal props were much more in evidence at this rehearsal. Nicole had already put a call out to a member of the Wardrobe to remove Xerxes' knighting sword, and a dresser passed me with Romilda and Atalanta's jackets which she was just about to hang on the backs of their chairs for the Library Scene.

'I've just been ironing their blouses,' she said. The door to the Running Wardrobe (just off the PS) was open and a gust of laundry and ironing smells filled the wing.

I spent most of Acts II and III sitting on the Generals' bench, which was parked OP US, with a fine view of Persepolis. I chose it because it was unbelievably comfortable after days on trucks (and in draughts), a view unfortunately held by the chorus as well who collapsed on it whenever they could. I say 'unfortunately' as it was in this rehearsal that a private artistic crisis came to a head. One of the drawbacks of being in the wings was that I had to draw in public and, overwhelmed by helpful suggestions, I began to consider total honesty in portraiture something of a mistake. That morning, surrounded by chorus and crew, I decided to scrap it – and not a moment too soon . . .

Jean Manning joined me.[4]

'Hallo Sarah,' she said. 'Are you revelling in it? I love this show.'

She leafed through the sketch book until she came to

her picture. 'Oh you are naughty. Where's my waist?'

Even Keziah was keeping a wary eye on her image.

'I can give you two minutes to draw me,' she said, as she prowled past on a Warden hunt.

'Oh yeah?' I replied, 'Which is your best side?'

'We could negotiate . . .'

Meanwhile on stage one of the Generals (Brian Casey) was winning the bowls match by actually hitting the jack, although somebody else's bowl must have come very near as *two* roars went up from the audience. Yvonne was in the OP wing as they exited (to thunderous applause).

'That was a stunning match,' she said, 'a classic.

And on she swept for the Quarrel Scene while the wing was hastily cleared of props and griffins and Bob fixed up the new arc light. The moment the Lovers had dashed past, he and the prop staff ran on to the stage and, masked by the hedge curtain, set the plinths and busts for the last scene, bolting the magic plinth to the floor and rolling Handel into the centre.

The show came to a triumphant close ten minutes later and (after the first call), Bob and his men were back on stage again to clear up the debris from the broken busts, zipping back smartly into the wings as the Hedge Curtain went up for the second call. The curtain calls were of course being rehearsed, the flymen, the door operators and the prop staff having as much to do as the singers; however, the applause was so enthusiastic that it felt very like the real thing. Indeed, some parts of the show had clearly been too effective. One of the audience was heard to say afterwards.

'I thought those grey people were ghosts . . . until they moved.'

The First Night, January 14th

The First Night itself was mysteriously less tense and more business-like. The Stage Door was snowed in with 'Good luck' cards but the canteen was full of singers and crew stolidly eating their supper and the only actual indication that we were about to do a performance tonight was the appearance of the orchestra in evening dress. This included even the offstage band who were set amongst the minute ruins of Persepolis.

Three of them, two recorders and a violin, were naturally in costume (they accompany Romilda's Concert Aria on stage) but the others were also in orchestral black[5] and even the guy who set up their music stands was wearing a DJ. Stephen Harris (the chorus master) was stationed at one of the TV trolleys, to conduct them, and further down the wing Amanda was just about to plunge us into darkness by asking someone to switch off the working lights. Before she did so, I noticed that she too was in evening dress and that Bob, checking the edges of the grass carpet, was in a DJ. I asked one of the Wardens, Mark Holmes, if this was in honour of the First Night.

'No,' he said, 'they always dress like that. Don't they do that at Covent Garden?'

'Not that I know of,' I said. 'They just dress in black sweatshirts and jeans. Although I think there's a DJ on hand somewhere in case someone has to go on with flowers.'

Mark shook his head, 'How tacky,' he said.

Bob appeared in the PS, anxious to demonstrate how hard you had to pull the silk drape that covers Xerxes' Bridge.

'You'd better tell Louise,' he warned Amanda, 'you really have to yank it – like this . . .'

And before anybody could stop him he had tugged the cord and revealed the whole thing.

'Working lights *on*,' said Amanda wearily.

'Gawd,' said the bloke who switched them on. 'Oh well, it'll be all right on the night.'

A message instantly came through from Jane, the lights were to be switched off (there were three minutes to go) and Amanda, leaving the Bridge until the Interval, ran a thoughtful torch beam over the Parterre. One of the nails was sticking out and she summoned Leroy Shortt (one of the stage crew) to bang it into place, followed by Harry Humphreys with some Tipp-ex to cover up the traces. One minute to go and the Wardens were with us, their heads shining slightly in the gloom.

‘’Ere, ’Arry,’ said somebody (and I’m sorry if it sounds quaint but it’s what he said).

‘You still got the Tipp-ex? Mike’s got some pink showing on ’is Barnet.’

An off-stage cellist stumbled into me at this point and asked where the back wall was. ‘It’s so difficult coming in from the light,’ she said, and actually the darkness was by now total. Even Persepolis and the music stands were blacked out. I directed her to her music stand and retired DS, behind the prop trolley.

Meanwhile the chorus were swarming on and Amanda had stationed herself at the US entrance. ‘Gentlemen!’ she said (which stopped the chatter for about two seconds), ‘I’m dishing out your sticks.’ Off they went on to the stage and the crew pushed the door to and left. Two chorus ladies ran in. ‘We’re locked out,’ said one, with no trace of mental disturbance – and they disappeared. A burst of applause told us that Ivor had reached the podium. ‘We’re off!’ said Laurie (on the PS door) and Amanda prepared to follow the Overture with her torch.

As Louise launched into her first aria, five Wardens lined up for their entrance – to set deckchairs – joined later by the sixth, Mark, who, hastily swapping the Spade for a pile of concert programmes, tagged on behind and disappeared through the DS door. Louise was followed by Yvonne and, as the Concert Aria filtered through the scenery, Amanda took stock of the amount of space in the wing. It obviously struck her that the exiting Wardens (plus deckchairs) would crash straight into the Parterre as soon as they came off the stage and she stationed herself by the door, with her right arm extended. The result of this manoeuvre was jolly impressive; the Wardens reappeared, marching steadily with chairs under their arms, nearly bumped into Amanda, looked thoughtfully at her arm and, without a flicker, executed a tight left turn and marched off US.

The wing was uncannily quiet and I assumed at the time that this was how people behaved during a performance, however it was probably only First Night nerves. Things eased up considerably as the run progressed; all of us were obviously listening anxiously to the audience since there was a general sigh of relief at the first round of applause (for '*No stain can blemish*').

The deckchair aria, '*When I see her,*' also got a good hand, much to the satisfaction of the stage management team, as it covered the noise of the flying deckchairs and Mike's chariot rumbling on for the Hedge Clipping Scene. The hedge curtain itself was in a frisky mood that night and bounced so alarmingly that Bob, creeping cautiously up the ladder behind Mike, ducked in alarm. His DJ looked particularly incongruous as he chucked the bits of green carpet over but his timing was perfect. The improbable pause, between the snip of Mike's shears and the appearance of the clipping, clearly delighted everybody and Nicholas Hytner's plea to reduce the gag to a throw-away quietly gave up the ghost.

Some of the Wardens were gathered round one of the US TV monitors, glaring at what members of the audience they could see on the screen. A seat behind the conductor is no place to be if you are at all sensitive to what people are saying about you.

'Look at that one,' Bob Smith was saying, 'he hasn't laughed all opera.'

'Which one? The skull?'

'No, the grave digger next to him.'

At which point the audience provokingly woke up and laughed at Mark Richardson's entrance – or rather at his self-satisfied beam as he marched on. I was told afterwards that he addressed the audience directly, which gave them the agreeable feeling that they were Ancient Persians; they were certainly in a very good mood by the time we reached the Interval and started clapping Nerys' aria '*By stealing secret kisses*' in the play-out.

In the Interval Mark told me that he'd added his beam to the audience after watching Ian Richardson address the camera in the '*To Play the King*' series on TV. He wasn't convinced that Julia would wear it.

Moving across to the OP for Act II, after the cramped conditions on the other side, felt like stumbling on to a prairie. The *Rosenkavalier* scenery had been taken down to LBH and the only things filling up the space were the *Fledermaus* stagecoach, the Plane Tree, any amount of grey shadow and Jane, methodically scouring its vast reaches with the aid of a pencil torch. As she came into hailing distance she asked me if I'd seen the jewel case. I hadn't, and on she went. The entire Act was punctuated by Bob and Jane continuing the search between cues, they were so very unfazed that I supposed there was an understudy ready.

The rest of Act II went very well: the cactuses came on and off, the weather synchronised with the Bridge's collapse and what little one heard of the singing sounded marvellous. However, by the Pillar Scene the jewels were still missing and Louise entered with a case hastily cobbled up by Props. Yvonne's appalled reaction to the substitute jewels came right through the scenery: in rehearsal she might have wondered if she should swap brothers but tonight she made up her mind instantly and returned the necklace with a decided '*No*, thank you.'

The last Act whizzed past. Halfway through, Bob brought the bouquets on and parked them, in buckets, by the cactuses, which gave one a new angle on the surprise and delight with which the ladies usually receive them.

The very last aria sounded so splendid that I ditched drawing and watched the last scene through a crack in the Hedge door. As I turned to move back I found the cue light already on Standby (for the Hedge) and the impassive stage management calmly waiting for me to move.

And suddenly it was all over. Everybody was in the wings looking extremely happy, kissing each other and slapping the back of the principals as they entered for their solo bows.

In came the Hedge, the ASMs dashed off to clear up the bust debris, out came the flowers, Louise brought on Ivor and suddenly the wing filled up with Dennis Marks and Others who swept the principals off. Coo, well, that's that, I thought, when a sudden jab of vegetation in the back of the neck made me turn round – and there was Jean beaming at me over her bouquet.

Notes

1 This is the Japanese expression for 'Good luck!' and used all over the world – although it appeared to hit England the moment the Royal Opera House came back from its first Japanese tour.

2 Some Italian houses put operas on in a block, a week of *Traviata*s, for example, and close the theatre a few days before the show so they can rehearse in the afternoon and evening. One assumes they are heavily subsidised.

3 This courtesy is extended to all conductors, apparently to make sure they get there.

4 A much loved member of the ENO chorus, famous for her solo dance in *Rigoletto* and for shaking her fist at the entire French Army in *War and Peace*.

5 Another violin, viola, cello, double bass and theorbo (archlute). There is a plan of the Pit and the offstage band on page 202.

14
The Running Wardrobe

Once an opera goes into performance the days suddenly empty. The cast, naturally, only appear on the days they are performing and other shows take up rehearsal time on the stage. I filled in the days between *Xerxes* visiting the other theatre departments, starting with the Running Wardrobe.

They live just off the PS wing, in a space that looks suspiciously as though it was originally intended to be a corridor; the high narrow room is lined with racks of costumes for the operas currently in the rep (the *Traviata* crinolines instantly oblige you to inch along sideways) and is generally filled with the pleasant smell of laundry. Washing and ironing go on in a sunken room behind the main one and above that, via a wooden ladder, is the office of the Running Wardrobe's manager, Ray Sheppard. He was dashing off somewhere but told me to look through the *Xerxes* box. 'We've had real problems with Arsamenes' jacket,' he added, and disappeared.

I noticed that he and his computer were only allowed a very small corner of the room, the rest being devoted to sewing machines and storage, but it was at least that rare thing among Coliseum offices, airy and light filled. Sitting down at one of the two huge desks of drawers that ran down the centre, I looked round for the *Xerxes* box. The left wall was covered with stacks of boxes containing stock stage accessories while ahead were the swatch boxes. A swatch is, of course, a sample of material and the swatches were arranged in colour order (red/orange/rust, for example) with a selection of hues tacked up beneath each box. The black swatches ran to three large boxes. Of course, there *are* lots of blacks but our

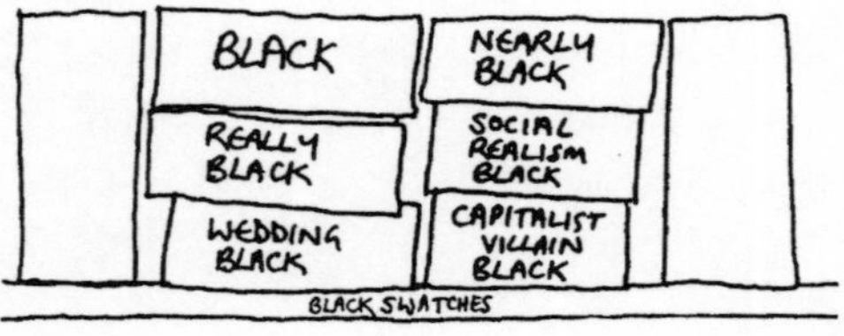

collection still looked like a legacy from the 1980s. I once talked to someone from the dyeing shop who had particularly vivid memories of that era.

'The worst thing,' she said, 'was the constant black – and having to put mud on 50 pairs of boots.'

'Which show was that?' I'd asked.

'*All* of them . . .'

The production boxes lived on a precarious shelf above the sewing machines. Each live show[1] rates a box and, on pulling down *Xerxes*, I discovered it was mostly full of work sheets which itemised each costume, who made it, what it cost, where the material came from, and so on. By using them, it was a simple business to work out how much material was needed to clothe Ann Murray, for example, for the first run of *Xerxes* and how much her costume cost.

The Running Wardrobe needs this information in case they have to adjust, or replace a costume and, turning from the original production, I could see that recent re-makes had run into problems. Not only had the prices gone up but some of the material was no longer available. The brocade for Arsamenes' jacket was now unobtainable and various swatches showed Ray's attempts to recreate the original golden sheen; the preferred one bearing the annotation '4·5 metres of oyster high style, £16 a metre, printed by Penny Hadwill and toned down with spray paint by me.'

Leafing through the other sheets, I noticed that Zeb's dictum – the more people there are on stage, the less you notice the quality of their clothes – applied even to buttons. Those on Amastris' uniform were supplied from The London Badge and Button Company whereas the Wardens had to make do with grey plastic. In the same way, social distinctions were remorselessly defined by costume fabrics. Xerxes, Arsamenes and Romilda gleamed in brocade and satin, Amastris and the Generals were clothed in sensible breeches of wool cotton and jackets of ready dyed facecloth, while the Chorus and Wardens were reduced to having much of their costumes (the dress shirts, wing collars, and ubiquitous T-shirts) supplied from stock. Even Amastris' black coat was of a coarser, bobblier texture than the similar garment worn by Arsamenes. The coarsest material (and the oddest supplier) was reserved for the Warden's gardening aprons: they were made of green tarpaulin and 'supplied by ENO van drivers'.

The Wardens' black court shoes also came from stock but everybody else's shoes were specially made by Anello's in Leicester Square, and swatches of sample leather were attached to all the sheets. Gloves were either specially made or bought from Selfridge's although the wearing of gloves in *Xerxes* has been slowly eroded over the years. Xerxes takes his on and off throughout the show but Romilda ditches hers after her first aria and Atalanta's extraordinary pair, complete with gauntlets (like pre-war motoring gloves) have completely disappeared.

At the back of the file were a couple of costume designs and one of those curiously murky photocopies, usually taken from a magazine, that get sent to the Wardrobe and Prop departments as a visual reference. In this case it appeared to be a lady with a cravat tucked into her jumper and was doubtless included to provide a guide to the exact construction of Xerxes' cravat.

A few memos, dating from the first run, completed the box. The first, from Isobel Hatton (responsible for PS props), was a list of the things that would be needed for the LBH rehearsals: long practice skirts, coats, swords and belts. Most of this would have come from stock as, unlike props, costumes and accessories are not usually available for studio rehearsals. Singers normally

rehearse at LBH in casual clothes, topped off with any garment they need to get used to, and it is not until the show moves to the stage that the phrase, 'in wigs and costumes as available' begins to turn up on the call sheets. (This suddenly struck me as rather odd, but see below.)

The second memo came at the end of the LBH rehearsals. Some extra props (and pockets to put them in) were wanted, and all Jean Rigby's knee-acting in Act II was taking its toll on her breeches.

Memo

Jan 29th, Isobel Hatton to Bill Strowbridge (Wardrobe Master)

A few things have cropped up . . .

1) Amastris (Jean Rigby) needs the following:
   A sword belt
   Pocket for coin in her first costume
   Knee pads for Act 2 Scene 1
   Dagger which should look very vicious and suitable for killing. If we are going to use the one we have had, please can you smooth all the rough bits away?
2) Elviro (Chris Booth-Jones) will need a pocket for a hip flask.
3) Does Xerxes have a sword? If so, with which costume? And could Miss Murray have a very nice handkerchief, please?
4) Can you let me know who, if anyone, wears hats?

Swords (and their maintenance) are included here because, lacking an Armoury, the Wardrobe supplies all the swords that are merely worn on stage. The cast of *Xerxes* might menace each other with swords and sword-sticks but their weapons remain purely decorative.

Xerxes' handkerchief never made it to the First Night and only one person ever wore a hat – Jean Rigby. What is more, she kept it on her head for most of the show. I asked Gillian Dixon, the Wardrobe Mistress, if hats had ever been mooted for the other characters, but all I got was an enigmatic eulogium on Jean.

'Oh, Jean's a trooper! She never complains.'

Coming down from Ray's room I bumped into Candida Butt, one of the Wardrobe Supervisors.

'Candida,' I said, 'why aren't costumes available until the show gets to the stage?'

Candida paused, clearly wondering where to begin.

'Well, really because the singers aren't available for fittings until rehearsals begin, so we have to use that time for making the costumes or copying them. But even if they were ready we wouldn't let them have the costumes to rehearse in. You'd have to have a member of the Wardrobe staff sitting in on the rehearsal, just to keep an eye on the frocks – and we simply can't spare anyone. You wouldn't believe what happens to rehearsal clothes. The sets are rough and unfinished and they have nails sticking out, and the floors are dusty. The real costumes would get ruined.'

'Do you fit the singers?' I asked. 'I thought that was the job of the Making Wardrobe.'

'Yes, it is, but they are basically concerned with new productions. We have got the revivals to get ready. It can be a nightmare. Look at *Pearl Fishers*, for example. We're trying to fit in Chorus fittings for these saris. They look such a simple garment but their length is crucial; they have to be fitted properly or they'll snag on the stage or in the wings.'

The saris were right next to the magnificent toreador costumes for *Carmen*. I held one up and, though the heaviness of stage costumes is proverbial, was amazed at the weight. Candida spread out the equally heavy cloak.

'They are wonderful, aren't they? They are real Spanish bull fighting costumes. Isn't it lovely material? We managed to get the workers to come over from Spain to make them. The trouble is, though, they aren't theatrical costumes; they'll only fit the guys they were made for.'

She turned the jackets out to reveal a strange padded lining, with not a seam in sight, the garment was quite unadjustable,

'We put some sweat pads in, but they can never be cleaned. The sequins are imbedded in the material. Look at this work.'

The whole jacket was encrusted in wonderful swirls of glitter.

'It's marvellous detail. We'd never be able to produce stuff like that,' she added generously. (This from the department that produced the *Rosenkavalier* frocks . . .)

Notes

1 A 'live' show is one in the repertory. One that we will not play again, in its current production, is 'dead'.

15
Front of House and a Bomb Scare

January 19th

On the second night I arrived early to watch the theatre being made ready for the show. There had been a rehearsal of *Rosenkavalier* in the morning and the change-over (from *Rosenkavalier* to *Xerxes*) had taken until 5.00 p.m. Now it was the turn of the LX to re-focus the lamps.

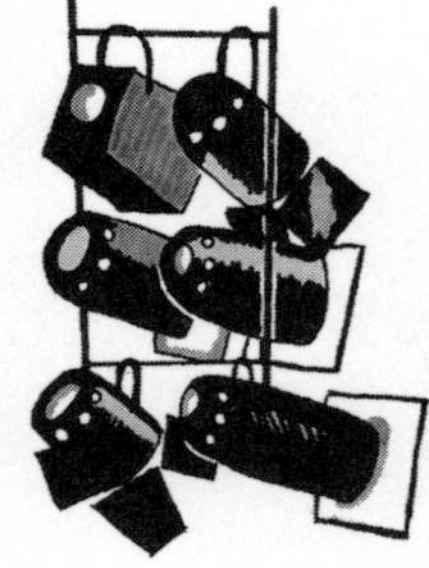

Most of the 400 or so lamps on the stage are hung on bars in the flies, however, once the set is up, the lamps cannot be brought down to stage level since the bars would bash into the scenery. Consequently, the LX techs have to climb up to refocus the lights and change the coloured gels and, as I got to the Dress Circle, Neville Currier (Electrics Supervisor) was directing operations.

All the House lights were off and the stage was lit by intermittent flashes as Neville asked Tom in the LX box to switch lamps on and off. They were talking to each other through walkie talkies and, as Tom's remarks were also being relayed through two large speakers at the front of the stage, the effect was rather uncanny. On stage the deck chairs and the grass carpet had been stacked up DS, on the netting over the Pit, and a chap called Len was being rolled round on a wheeled ladder by four members of the crew. I could see nothing of him but a leg. The rest of him was presumably entangled in the lighting bar above the stage, and the others called out, 'Hang on, Len!' every time they moved him.

Neville was apparently conducting the proceedings from the list of lamps he had in his hand, but actually by heart; the lamps are all numbered and Neville not only appeared to know each one but also the exact colour and direction of each lamp for the show. Every one of his instructions was a variation of '205, please' (it was switched on) 'Tighten it slightly please, Len' (a wobble of light) 'Drop it a bit, please' (another wobble) 'Okay, kill that' (it was turned off) 'Thank you.'

I learnt that lamp number 65 lights up the OP grass, 66 the PS Grass, 67 PS US and 69 Handel himself. One of the LX guys told me later that our circuitry is absolutely fixed by number and that you get used to it. 208, for example, is bound to be DS OP. Even so it was a virtuoso performance.

They started changing some of the gels.

'190 and 189 are white,' said Neville, and a couple of redundant blue gels floated down. Len was pushed a little further along the bar. 'You can lose those colours as well,' (down came two yellow gels) 'we've lost that show for ever.' I don't know what the unpopular show was, but a couple of the crew said, 'Hurray,' and one guy even clapped his hands.

The Tree was wheeled into position, so they could check that the spotlight was hitting it correctly, and a painter – touching up the white paint on the scenery – took this opportunity to tidy up its pot, unobserved.

'Blimey,' said one of the crew a moment later (wiping the fresh paint off his hands), 'you leave the Tree for a moment and some guy paints it.'

Neville looked at the chap's white trousers. 'Yup, I wouldn't stand there too long if I were you.' But the painter had already moved off and was climbing up some scaffolding to paint over the joins in the side flats.

The Flys were clearly on call as the Pillars, the Hedge Curtain and the back wall were brought in and out, to make sure they were lit correctly, and by 6 p.m. David Groves, the Head Technician, was on stage, gauging how much Neville had to do, and politely hurrying him up.

A couple of crew heaved the grass carpet off the net and began to hoover it while Neville's chaps flitted around the stage picking up discarded gels, just ahead of another couple of techs with stage brooms. Neville had himself disappeared backstage to go through the lamps in the wings (they throw a raking beam on the rain and the Persepolis mountains) and the lamps on the stage itself. These latter are concealed by 'Groundrows' – a term that has described low-level scenery since the seventeenth century. Groundrows traditionally conceal lights on the stage and in *Xerxes* they mask lamps that light up the desert with suitable colours: pale red, orange and dark blue.

Neville finished by running through the weather slides; the projector had been set at a tilt and the clouds appeared to be rushing downhill and, while he was sorting this out, Jane Randall had the Winged God run in a couple of times and made sure that the grass carpet was tucked in neatly beneath the white walls. At 6.06 David said with much relief, 'Okay boys' and brought in the Hedge Curtain.

For the past half hour the harpsichord tuner had been working on both harpsichords in the pit (they were to take him another half hour), and the pleasant sound of plucked strings was joined by rattling chains as the exit doors began to be opened. Richard Woodeson (Deputy House Manager) ambled on to the stage, looked into the void, blew a whistle – and suddenly the auditorium was full of ushers.

They called out their names, level by level, and scattered to various exits for Emergency drill. From all over the empty House came the sound of firm reassuring voices: 'This way please ladies and gentlemen. Use all available exits. Please go directly to the nearest exit,' and so on. The audience itself was obviously about to come in and I got up to go, just as a girl from Catering appeared in a Dress Circle box. She covered the little table at the back with flowers and a couple of champagne buckets, while some clinks from the Dress Circle indicated that an invisible colleague was setting up the Bar out there. The Stalls Promenade was already full of the smell of freshly brewed coffee.

Once in the OP, I crammed a chair just by the first DS entrance – which is never used in this opera (but see below) – and found Ivor Bolton waiting to be taken down to the pit.

'Hi, it's an exciting night tonight,' he said.

'Is it?' I said.

'It certainly is, Blackburn are playing Portsmouth.'

The Overture started at 7.05. Nicole was on the Book and I watched her cue and Ivor's opening beat to see which went first – I couldn't work it out. In a quiet patch, she told me that her first cue is to Ivor and the Flys simultaneously (to bring up the curtain). However, Ivor takes no notice of it so she has got into the habit of switching on the green light when the stage is ready, and leaving him to start in his own time.

'It makes it awkward,' she said, 'because I'm supposed to give the flying cue on his upbeat. But I'm used to him now and I can tell when he's going to start.'

I looked at the monitor. He makes a sort of preliminary waggle before he begins a piece.

While she was explaining this, somebody from Wardrobe arrived, looking as if she was expected.

'Somebody wants something steaming,' she said.

'Eh?' said Nicole.

'I was told to come here,' said the lady, 'to steam something.'

'Well, I'll put a call out,' said Nicole dubiously. 'Anybody want something steaming?'

Kindly suppressing Jane's immediate response, 'Bob's pants.' (which naturally just came through the headset), Nicole was just about to go into the matter more thoroughly when Kate Littlewood (the House Manager) appeared in a state of controlled agitation.

'We've got to stop the show,' she said, 'we have to evacuate the building now.'

Nicole meditated for about half a second and then, very methodically, began to go through all her channels telling Jane, the Flys, the PS and so on that the show was about to be stopped. Nobody was impressed. 'Oh gawd,' said Amanda. 'Why?' said the Flys, while Jane bore down on the prompt desk to find out what on earth the trouble was and whether the backstage areas were affected.

Kate meanwhile was thirsting to get on stage and empty the theatre – and it suddenly struck me that my chair and I were blocking up the entrance that she was plainly determined to use. I hastily turned myself into a small unsuspicious package and Kate walked on.

Chris Robson said afterwards that it took several seconds for anybody on stage to register what was happening.

'Hello, there's Kate,' he remembered thinking. 'I wonder what she's doing here?'

Ivor stopped the band and Kate asked the audience to leave the theatre as quickly as possible. The audience appeared to be just as disgruntled as Amanda. 'Oh gawd,' they said to a man and trundled obediently off to the exits.

Backstage Nicole had to alert the rest of the building, she pulled the Tannoy towards her and said, 'We are having to evacuate the theatre. Would you all leave the building as quickly and quietly as possible.'

People simply downed tools and went while Nicole agonised over her impromptu announcement. 'Quickly and quietly, indeed, why did I say that? It comes straight from school.'

I thought it sounded very reassuring.

Of course, while she was doing this she *wasn't* cueing the back wall doors for Romilda's exit, and Yvonne, her back to Kate and the stirring events downstage, was clearly wondering why she couldn't get off. Next minute the Iron[1] was down (Nicole had summoned the Fireman) and the whole cast was in the wings asking intelligent questions ('What's going on?' principally) which just goes to show that the last people to know what's happening in an emergency are the people on stage. *They* don't hear the stage announcement (they are too bewildered by the opera grinding to a halt round them) and they arrive in the wings too late to hear the other message from the Prompt Corner.

Chris said he supposed it was a bomb warning.

'Aha' said Louise, 'Do we go back to our dressing rooms?'

'No, out of the building apparently,' said Yvonne, and the three of them disappeared.

MAY'S COURT
Reminds me of the old campaign against the Medes..

The rest of us trooped out of the Stage Door and were begged to stand away from the theatre. The audience naturally came round the back to admire the cast and chorus and I found myself next to the chorus lady I'd stood next to in a *War and Peace* bomb alert years ago. She said these occasions were worse if you were doing a show like *Iolanthe*, all that flimsy netting (and she'd once left her wings behind in a café); even so, the costumes did not look over warm. Typically, Mark Richardson had had his anorak and scarf to hand and put them on over his General's greatcoat.

One of the audience said, afterwards, that she'd seen all the ENO staff swoop out of the stage door and go left, except the gorgeously dressed Xerxes, Arsamenes and Romilda who'd gone right. Stage Management would have welcomed this information twenty minutes later when the show was due to restart and they couldn't account for the three main singers. Rumour had it that, after a major panic, they were eventually discovered in a coffee bar but actually they re-appeared at just the right moment and the coffee was a frightful calumny.

'We were having a Perrier,' said Chris.

We streamed back into the warm in high spirits, one of the Generals saying in Blimpish tones, 'Shockin' fuss. In the War, y'know, we used to carry on.'

While Noel Davis called out, 'Okay, where shall we start? Act III?'

Actually we started at the Investiture and sent Dennis Marks (the General Director) on to tell the audience the bits of the story they were going to miss.

By this time Stage Management had corralled the cast, changed the set and kept an anxious eye on how the auditorium was filling up. The canteen was full of half-eaten suppers (I hope they all got a free re-fill). Everyone I met congratulated me on being in tonight. 'That's a nice cartoon for you,' they said generously. Much later we heard that the cause of all the fuss had been a suspect package in the cloakroom. A couple of ROH colleagues shook their heads in the Interval over ENO's way of managing things. At the Garden, they assured me, the House Managers were accustomed to pick up suspect packets, run with them into Bow Street and then phone the local police – whose problem it now was.

Anyway, our show went on and, once the Generals and the Winged God had entered successfully, Jane came past to congratulate Nicole on her handling of the incident. Nicole said that Dennis had congratulated her as well.

The race was now on to finish by 10.30 . . . or to be landed with a huge bill for overtime. The stoppage had lasted from 7.19 to 7.45 and in starting at the Investiture Jane and Nicole reckoned they'd saved on 15 minutes worth of music; but how to make up the other 11 minutes? During Romilda's '*If You'd Seduce Him*' Julia phoned through from the Front of House to see if the first Interval could be reduced to 15 minutes, which would give us an extra five and, when this was put hastily to the orchestra and chorus representatives, they very decently agreed to have *both* intervals shortened. This left us with one minute to knock off, which Ivor felt could be safely left to him. 'At Glyndebourne,' he said, 'It was sometimes so tight that I couldn't bring the orchestra to their feet at the end of the opera. We reckoned the show was over when their bottoms hit the seats, and an extra 15 seconds sometimes made all the difference.'

As the Rainbow aria, '*The love cross'd by fortune*' heralded the end of Act II, Nicole commented that it was lucky we didn't put the House lights on in the 'B' section nowadays. 'They'd probably all evacuate the Theatre again.' We both studied the monitor. The Stalls were looking rather quiet and unnerved.

Act III started off with the Egg case bumping alarmingly over the DS floorboards and crashing into the edge of the carpet. Two shoves from Mike and it was over but it had left a couple of huge rucks behind and Nicole quickly called up Amanda. 'You'd better tell the bowls team that the carpet has got rucked. No, hold on . . .' For on stage, Chris, in the middle of his row with Romilda, had moved US and was stomping the carpet down, apparently in a fit of absent-minded fury. 'Chris has sorted it out. He's such a star, isn't he?'

During the next aria, however, the Wardens watched him with rather less enthusiasm. They were gathered round the monitor to see what Chris was doing to their deckchairs ('*Ah love, tyrannic love*' is a bad moment to be a deck chair) and were appalled to see that he was in one of his risk-taking moods: singing his aria sitting on the floor and flailing about in the middle of them.

'That's mine, stuck in the middle,' said one. Crash! 'Yeah, well, there goes yours.'

'Hi!' said another indignantly, 'He's f—ing eating mine.'

The Quarrel Duet was suddenly upon us, the wing was clear, the arc light on, Yvonne and Chris thundered past ('Phew,' we thought), when from behind the black drape we heard a clear soprano voice say, 'Door!' There was a sort of a whoosh and they were on stage just in time.

Nicole looked up placidly, 'Didn't you see the cue light, Phil?'

'I was pushing the US edge,' said Phil mysteriously, while another chap sidled round. 'It was *my* fault' he said and there the matter rested. I can't imagine what he'd done.

***

During the duet the audience showed definite signs of waking up. 'A fine time,' grumbled Bob, and the curtain calls were punctuated by whoops and whistles. In the wings the cast seemed a little taken aback by the sudden enthusiasm but clearly felt that the audience had redeemed themselves.

'There are a lot of yellers in tonight,' said Chris indulgently.

Ivor told me that Blackburn had won, 3–1.

Back in the dressing room Gaby Castillo, one of the dancers, told me another theatre bomb story. She had been in the ROH *Escalramonde*, 'With one of those Australian Dames.' (A Woosterism sprang immediately to mind, 'Specify, old fruit, there are so many . . .') Anyway, she agreed it was probably Dame Joan Sutherland, and there the Dame was 'All six feet of her, and there was me and my friend Sue on each side as handmaids. We were waiting to go on and up came the Stage Manager, walking on eggshells as she got near this Dame, and she went straight up to her – not even looking at us – and said 'Dame Whatever-her-name-was, I must ask you to follow me now to No 45, there is a bomb scare,' and off they walked, and me and Sue were just left standing there, staring at each other. "What do we do?" said Sue, "wait until we blow up?"'

The ROH contingent, when I met them later, immediately endorsed this story as very probable indeed.

Note

1 The Safety Curtain, actually an Iron, is either In (down) or Out (up).

16
The Sound Department

All this talk of explosions encouraged me to go round to the Sound Box to talk to Lucy Paget, one of the Sound Engineers.

She and her colleagues share half of the old Royal Box at the back of the Stalls with the Lighting Department. The light levels there are so dim, and the technicians so quiet, that most of the audience are unaware of them; however, there is evidence of the department slung all round the auditorium. A tangle of aerials juts out over the lamps in the front of the Dress Circle, speakers climb up each side of the proscenium arch and a couple of mikes hang over the stage from the ceiling.

All this looks extremely suspicious in an opera house and the first thing I asked Lucy was whether we miked the singers. 'On the whole, not,' was the reassuring reply. She took me through the equipment we could see.

The aerials were for radio mikes. These *might* be fitted to a performer (a child, for example) but they were also used for communications. Most of the departments backstage speak to each other on walkie-talkies wired up with headsets, a particularly useful device for people, like the Flys, who need to keep their hands free. The walkie-talkie has several channels and Stage Management (for example) cue other departments on the public channel, while reserving a private one to talk amongst themselves.

The bulk of the hardware in the auditorium is there to take the sound of the opera around the House. The music has to be relayed to the Limes box, the Flys, the LX box, the wings and (far backstage) to the canteen and the dressing rooms. It even has to be taken up to the stage, as each show has its own acoustic dead spots (US usually) where the singers cannot hear the pit. The only amplified sounds the *audience* hears are sound effects, offstage music and a discreet boost for early instruments like theorbos.[1]

Lucy said the lute in *Xerxes* had to be amplified for the audience

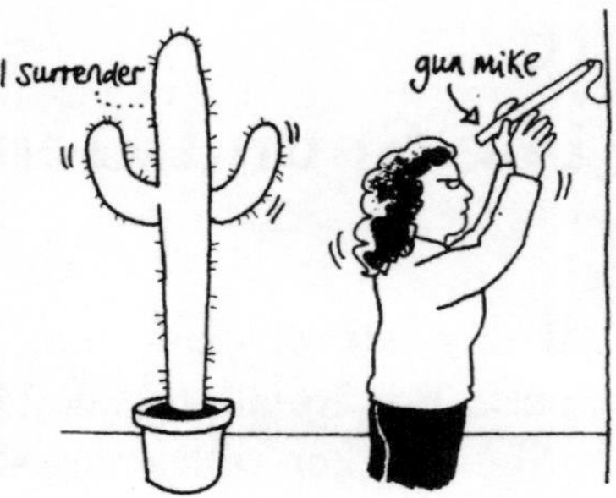

and the conductor. 'We use a gun mike to pick it up,' she added.

'A what?'

'It's a directional mike that looks rather like the barrel of a gun. It just picks up what it's pointed at. The sound comes out of the lute speaker which I lean up against one of the harpsichord legs. That way Ivor can hear the sound before it escapes into the auditorium. The singers can't hear the continuo instruments so we mike them as well. Of course, the sound is only relayed to the stage.' (See illustration 14)

'Is the offstage band miked?' I asked.

'No it isn't and I bet you can't hear it.'

'I've never heard it out front. In fact I was amazed to find it existed.'

'Oh well, you should see what we do with the band in *Rosenkavalier*.'[2]

The Sound Department does not normally become active in a production until the opera begins to be rehearsed in-house.

'Of course a producer might tell us in advance what sound effects (FX) he's looking for – but you can't do very much until the show is on stage. We have to hear *exactly* how it sounds.'

And once the Sound FX have been sorted they have to be cued.

'Actually all the cues come from the Prompt Corner but some effects have to be in time with the stage action – like the sound of a champagne cork. Here at the back of the Stalls we're usually in a much better position to see the show than the Prompt so though they *give* us the cue, they let us go in our own time.'[3]

One of the problems of the tight ENO rehearsal schedule was that the Sound Department never had a straight sound rehearsal; so they try out the FX when they can, usually when the singers aren't singing. I told Lucy about the terminal shock I'd recieved when the thunderclap burst from the Flys during the Stage and Piano rehearsal.

'Oh, yes. That explosion is new. It was put together by a student we had working for us last month.'

For a minute I had a vision of the youngster exploding things on waste land somewhere, his tape recorder at the ready, but a moment's reflection convinced me that he had used pre-existing sound material.

Lucy told me that the odd thing about sound effects was that real things often don't sound the way we think they should. 'Practically the only thing that does,' she said, 'are horses' hooves.'

Most other effects have to be cooked up. They had to create the noise of breaking bones, for example, in *Princess Ida* last season, and Lucy discovered that the sound of celery, broken very slowly and horribly (and amplified) was completely disgusting.

'That was a major triumph.'

And what about miking the voice, did we really never do it?

'Basically, no. We might relay offstage choruses, simply because of the heavy scenery you get nowadays, but this theatre is all about beautiful sound and we'd have to have a fantastic system to show off the trained voice. We haven't got it, and the singers don't need it.'

'What about oracles and ghosts and things?'

'Oh, people can't resist fiddling with *them*. In our last *Don Giovanni* the ghost had a radio mike on with the reverberation up. It made him sound very ghostly. It's really children you need radio mikes for. We're using them for the kids in *Rosenkavalier* at the moment.'

Looking round the Sound Box and seeing the tape deck, I asked Lucy if they taped the shows. 'Only for internal use,' was the reply, although 'I had to make a one-off tape for the Signer[4] last year, so he could learn the whole opera – repeats and everything. He was amazing. He acted all the parts and when the explosion happened he threw his arms up in the air.'

Looking at the formidable controls of the sound console in

front of me, I nearly repeated this useful gesture, but we both agreed that I'd have more chance of understanding the Sound Box if I returned, during a performance, and watched it in operation.

Notes

1 The theorbo or archlute is very noticeable in *Xerxes* as its great stem sticks out above the orchestra pit; backstage it is referred to simply as 'the lute'.

2 I did, see page 154.

3 These are called 'visual' cues – shortened to 'vis' on the cue sheets.

4 Many ENO performances are signed for the hard of hearing.

17
Quick Changes and the Stage Crew

January 21st

I started the evening in the canteen queue with Mark Holmes and Lucy. The risotto I had chosen set Mark reminiscing about the Russian tour and he told us that the Moscow crew had swept up the rice after the storm scene and taken it away in bags, presumably to sift and cook.

'Have you noticed,' said Lucy conversationally, 'how the canteen has given us rice every night since *Xerxes* has been on?'

Looking up at the TV monitor we were surprised to see, given the lateness of the hour (6.35 and the show due to start at 7.00) that the stage still being set; I thankfully discarded my supper and went up.

The fireman had just lowered the Iron. The 11 tons of iron blocks cut out the sound of the stage so effectively that the audience can be allowed in while the set is still being built; and tonight the crew, secure in the Iron's sound-proofing qualities, continued to bang down the carpet and roll the Winged God until 6.59. Brian shook his head as he passed, 'That *Rosenkavalier* change-over . . .' he grumbled. As usual people were walking unconcernedly about the stage as things flew in and out, though the sudden appearance of the back wall (a heavy French flat[1]) did cause a flurry of 'Heads! Heads up!' One bloke walked under it with nothing on his mind except his hair. 'Heads up, Ray' said another guy reproachfully; Ray shook his head, you could see he was thinking it wouldn't dare . . .

Over in the Prompt Side Laurie was fiddling with the Bridge. 'Do you want to see how it works?' he said – and collapsed it totally. I was aghast at the destruction but he said that Amanda had wanted him to check it out and, in fact, she appeared at this moment to view the wreckage. The Bridge turned out to be a simple mechanical prop: the handle on the side releases a plate of metal which keeps the base of the Bridge up. Once that goes, everything follows it. Pulling up the two handles on the side clicks everything back in place. As I tried to draw the mechanism, I was aware of a rather tense silence and, looking up, I caught Amanda's eye.

'Do you mind if I turn the working lights off now, Sarah?' she said.

Well, nobody wants 'Opera held for cartoon' entered in the stage sheet,[2] so I decamped hastily to the LX stairs, where there is always a patch of light, and found another member of the stage crew messing around with light bulbs. He rather set the pattern for the whole evening by insisting on thumbing through my sketch pad.

'Listen,' he said. 'When you are giving one of your tours, I hope you tell them it's a Bastard Prompt.'

'I usually call it a Squint Prompt,' I said.

'No, you should use the right word. Don't you worry about the school kids – they ought to know what a little basket is.'

It was 6.59 and the noise on stage seemed to be dying down. As I went over to the OP (via the passage between the dressing rooms and the back of the stage), I could hear Yvonne on my right, practising the Concert Aria in her dressing room while, uncannily, the stage violinist rehearsed the same music on my left; they couldn't hear each other.

At 7.01 pm we were all clear, Jane wrote a laconic 'v. tight' on the stage sheet and Ivor appeared in the Prompt Corner ready to be taken into the Pit. Behind me a couple of Wardens were doing some early audience spotting, 'Look at that one. He's asleep already,' while Louise passed me with her customary buffet.

We were entertaining a stage management student that evening and I found her looking sadly at the wall of flats.

'This is not a show to see from the wings really, is it?' she said.

'Well, the PS is the side to be,' I said loyally, 'especially in Act II. It's got the Cake.'

She looked rather dubious. 'Yes, I've been told that,' she said.

Blimey, I thought, how much excitement does she want?

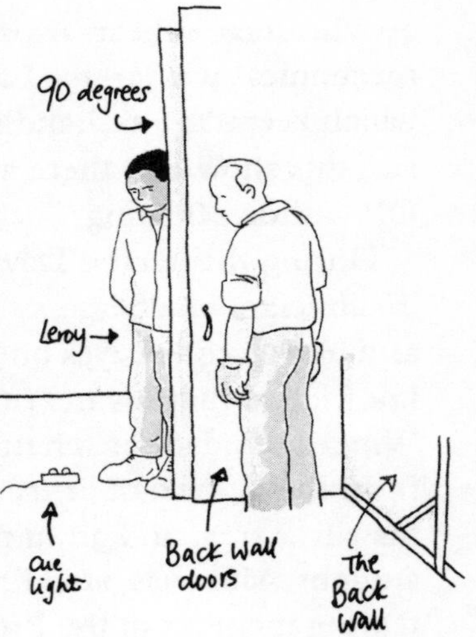

Chris demanded an update on the cartoons at this moment and, quite unwittingly, caused me to make my first (and last) Noise Off. Once the reverberations of the dropped sketch book had ceased to thunder through the wing, I went to sit on the Winged God platform to pull myself together and watch Yvonne and Jane set up the Concert Aria entrance. They were both keeping an eye on the TV monitor for Ivor's cue and, as the first '*Oh Hark!*' floated through the wing, Jane moved swiftly to the centre doors to give the operators a verbal 'Go!' Meanwhile Yvonne had assumed her Baroque position (see photo 'The Concert Aria'), beamed at the rest of us, turned this into a radiant smile for the king and, as the doors opened (simultaneously and at 90 degrees), disappeared on to the stage.

There is always a crowd US at this point and one of them turned out to be Leroy, a chap I'd met during the bomb scare. He told me he'd been an actor for a while but he preferred backstage work.

'I love this place,' he said. 'You can pick up quite a few trades if you work here.'

I asked him about something that had been puzzling me. Was there a designated gang of stage hands for each show?

'No,' he said, 'we do all the shows. The Head Technician[3] sorts out the daily lists for the shows and rehearsals and most guys are given set positions for the evening. But there is always one floating around, as a stand-by, who could be asked to do anything.'

'So you can all turn your hand to any bit of an opera?'

'Yup.'

'When do you learn it?'

'Well, sometimes we learn it all in the Dress Rehearsal but there are the stage rehearsals of course and a couple of technicals and sometimes we go to LBH. That's not very helpful, actually, because you're not handling the real things. You need 11 guys to run this show and there are usually three prop staff. One PS, one OP and one floating.'

During this recital David Groves, the Head Technician in charge of *Xerxes*, loomed up and narrowed his eyes but Leroy, secure in the knowledge that his next task was to open the Winged God door, chatted on. Mark exited from the Concert Scene, anxious to get rid of his silver tray, and attempted to give it to the student who was standing where any God-fearing member of the Prop staff should have been; he apologized profusely when he realised she didn't know what was going on.

'Stand still for a minute in the wings,' he said, 'and somebody will hand you something.'

Jane was at this moment removing a non-period plastic chair from behind the back wall and making sure that the two operators had folded back the wall's hinged supports so that would lie flush with the flat and fly out neatly for Atalanta's entrance. Brian joined me as I watched them and I asked him if the Russian rice story was true.

'You bet,' he said, and thus launched he told me how he could set the *Xerxes* set blindfold as a result of the Russian tour. Very few of the Russian theatres had provided anything like adequate staff and the skeleton crew ENO had taken out frequently found themselves setting the whole show.

'One afternoon the Russians sloped off after 30 minutes and left me stranded on the top of the scenery, but usually they didn't even turn up. There was one theatre where I worked for three days solid, setting and striking shows, and I was just beginning to feel really rough when Anne Murray and Yvonne Kenny marched into the wings and loaded me up with hot coffee and sandwiches. They're a lovely pair.'

I joined the student in the PS wing for Act II. Mark was looking with disdain at the cakes. 'They used to come from Patisserie Valerie in Old Compton Street,' he said, 'It's Tesco's now.'

Much of the Cake Scene was spent discussing the ladies' frocks with one of the Chorus. The *Xerxes* ones were bad enough she thought, tight across the ribs and under the armpits but the *Lohengrin* ones were a nightmare.

'They're so heavy that once you start moving on the *Lohengrin* stage,' (this is very steeply raked) 'they acquire a life of their own and drag you DS. *Rosenkavalier* has cheered us all up again. The frocks are made of really good material and beautifully cut. You can tell the Wardrobe enjoyed making them.'

I was due US, talking of the Wardrobe, to see the quick change before the Cactus Scene. Keziah had told me not to miss it and there I found that the solitary girl (trampled over during the second Stage-and-Piano rehearsal) had turned into seven people from Wardrobe and Make up, all ready to pounce with gardening aprons and ready-whitened sponges.

'You can feel the tension mount, can't you?' said Keziah.

The Wardens dashed up as she spoke, and, throwing the loops of the aprons over their heads, tried to get past Keziah and her mates as they covered up the skid marks on the top of their heads. Next minute they were in solemn lines behind the back wall, cactuses in hand.

Keziah re-appeared at the beginning of the Pillars Scene. She and the others, she said, had been ordered to stand by on stage for any Warden that needed a second coat – which was all very well but the Wardens were proving most elusive.

'They're making sure they keep out of my way. None of them wants an extra layer of slap.'

She pulled out a comb. 'Still, I wouldn't want them to think I wasn't ready.'

For Act III I was back PS and heard from Amanda that Louise was not very well. We listened with some anxiety to '*I go in certain hope*,' but her malaise didn't seem to be affecting her performance.

Her mind clearly at rest, Amanda alarmingly sat herself down and insisted on going through the whole of my pad, pencil sketches and all. As her torch relentlessly scrolled down each page I was in agony that she, and the PS door keeper (Laurie) who'd joined us, would miss a cue and vast portions of the show were consumed as I listened in horror for possible PS exits. But, of course, Amanda and Laurie were much more on the ball than me. 'Quick, Laurie,' she'd say, while wrestling with a caption, and he'd open the door just before Elviro broke his nose on it.

Over in the OP, Nicole was about to make one of the epic *Xerxes* calls. 'Your call please, Mr Richardson, ladies and gentlemen of the Chorus, the Generals, lady and gentlemen actors. Stand by please, Technicians for the Hedge doors and Prop Technicians for the Statues.'

She was obliged to say all this while Andy continued to chat blithely to her through the headset, and her desperation not to corpse came across loud and clear. Bob and Jane looked up to grin and, for the second call, they lent on the prompt desk to see if she'd make it through to the end. The announcement was a miracle of tottering control. 'You bastards!' cried Nicole, when she'd stopped gasping and – even then – she remembered to turn off the Tannoy; people's ability to remember which switches are on or off staggers me.

She, too, grabbed my sketch pad and, deprived of my natural occupation, I wandered off (I think with some idea of inspecting the OP wing, just cleared for the Quarrel Duet). At this moment even Nicole's iron nerve snapped.

'Sarah, stay here!' she said, putting quite a lot of emphasis on it (if you know what I mean) and, as I froze, there was a sound of running feet, a blue whirr, and the two lovers had thundered past me through the OP door. I never came so near to dabbing my forehead in my life.

Everybody in the wing stopped to listen to '*Rise ye Furies*' and, satisfied that Louise was in fine old form, gathered round the monitor to watch her smash the busts. The last one made a valiant effort to defy gravity and swung at an impossible angle for a second.

'What's happening?' came over the headset from Jane.

'It's deciding,' said Nicole dispassionately – CRASH!

Suddenly the show was over and the cast were in the wings, hugging each other and congratulating Louise. Yvonne swept her up, 'Well done, Louise, really well done.'

There was a roar from the audience as the principals went on again.

'It was obviously a marvellous performance,' said the stage management student wistfully.

Notes

1 A cloth that is mounted on a rigid framework is a French flat or a Frenchman; the call to 'Hang the Frenchman' is a venerable Flys joke.

2 A report on all the technical aspects of the show; one is completed for every performance.

3 He is called a Stage Supervisor nowadays.

18
The Stage and the Crew

The next day Brian Kinsey and I had coffee and to my delight I discovered he was at the famous Nicholas Hytner party.

Nicholas gave a supper party for the cast and production team before the first *Xerxes* rehearsals and everybody who was there tells you a different story of what happened. The most harrowing came from Nicholas himself who told a Friends of ENO meeting that he'd dropped a crucial bit of the supper in the kitchen and, while he and Ann Murray were picking it up, the singers had *roamed* his flat. They'd fetched up in his study, which was covered with little cards itemising the *Xerxes* moves.

Brian had been immensely impressed.

'He'd really done his homework,' he said. 'I was amazed. All round the walls he'd pinned hundreds of little postcards with every move in *Xerxes* plotted on them. Everything, "she'll turn her head right", every move. I've never known a producer work as hard as that. It really simplified the rehearsals.'

'He asked me later about all the things he wanted to do and though he didn't always agree with the things I said, you felt he was saying, "Fair enough." He asked me about the rain, and I said right away, "What you want is rice in a snow bag. We did that in *Night in Venice*" and he said, "Show me," so I got some muslin, made slits in the cloth, spread half a pound of rice along the middle and woggled the sides [all over the carpet presumably] and he loved it. He's a great bloke to work with, he knows how a show happens and understands what everybody on stage and backstage actually does. Jonathan Miller's like that too.'

Of course, not all Brian's work can be pre-planned in such detail. I asked him how he and his colleagues coped with the different operas in the repertory.

'Do you ever get shows in the rep that can't be fitted in the theatre?' I asked.

Brian gave me a look.

Aknathen Change-Over

'And how,' he said. 'In one season we'd lost three lorries and we were stacking scenery along the outside of the theatre, packing it in the wings and there was only about a foot clearance in the PS. We couldn't even set the cyc [the cyclorama] because we couldn't get enough space behind it to set the lights. We've had some really tight moments.'

'What about *Aknathen*?' I said, thinking of its notorious sand pit set.

'Yeah, that was difficult. Four tons of sand that show used, *eight* tons when it was wet. You could see the stage creaking from out front. *And* we had to shovel it up to set *Aida* . . .'

We moved away from this distressing topic to the Flys. I asked him about the nets looped under the Fly Gallery and learnt that they were there not for tumbling flymen, as I thought, but for errant counterweights. All flown scenery is counterweighted and, as the weights have to match the weight of the scenery, they are very heavy indeed.

'I've seen a weight fall from the Flys, bounce three times across the stage and smash straight into the OP side. And there was one that just plummeted from the gallery and buried itself in the PS floor. We had to cut away the floor to get it out, you can still see the patch.'

I began to see why red lights flash outside the doors to the stage when people are working above, in the Flys or the grid.

'What actually is the grid?' I asked. 'I mean, apart from the slatted floor above the Flys.'

'You should go up. We stack the motor for the heavy lifting machinery there, and all the wire systems from the flying equipment end up there.'

'Is there any particularly heavy stuff in *Xerxes*?'

'Yes, we store the *Xerxes* show pros[1] and its back arch up in the

Flys, just to get them out of the way. The back arch is really heavy as the side headers are attached to it. We take them off when the show is packed up.'

We continued our mental tour of the area above the stage. 'There's a bridge behind the pros, which is just used by Electrics, and another one in the OP. That can go up a metre if we've got a particularly tall bit of scenery to move. Then there's the Haystack above the grid.'

The Haystack is the glass-framed tower that covers the stage area. It is built to collapse outwards if the stage goes up in flames, creating an air current that ensures the fire goes *up* instead of spreading out. That's the theory, anyway. There is a Coliseum legend that a knife used to hang up there. Some of the frame is secured with rope and the idea must have been that a gallant Flyman shinned up there, cut the rope, saved the theatre, and got fried to a crisp.

We returned to *Xerxes*.

'The show needs 18 men to run it,' said Brian, 'Four Prop staff, ten techs and four Flymen. Two to pull the ropes, one on the stay rope and one to give the orders. What happens is, the supervisor dishes out all the jobs beforehand and you learn the show, as you go, in the stage rehearsals. Actually, once you've worked on a show, you never really forget it. I hadn't done *Russalka* for years and when I had to set it in Rome last year it all came flooding back.'

That reminded me that *Xerxes* had been all round the world.

'Have you been on many *Xerxes* tours?'

'Well, the Russian, of course. And the Brazilian, that was a nightmare. Their theatre had a raked stage which meant some of the doors had to be sliced off at the bottom (they still are) and the slope ruined the bowls game. But the worse thing was they didn't have any cue lights. Jane refused to run the show unless they got some, and even then it didn't really work. You couldn't get the Brazilians to understand what 'Stand-by' meant. As soon as a light came on they went. That made life fairly hairy. It was okay as long as everybody's reactions stayed hair-trigger and nothing went wrong.'

I asked about stacking the shows and the change-over. Did the Supervisor work that out before each day?

'He does if he's done his Homework. It really is called Homework. I've known some supervisors not bother and that's when we get trouble. The lads don't like hanging about – and scenery gets packed away all over the place.'

(Oddly enough, a later *Xerxes* performance illustrated the dire results of packing things away in a hurry.)

'*Xerxes* takes about four and a half hours to strike which means that if the stage is needed first thing the next day, we have to have an NCO (a Night Change Over). It takes just as long to build, as you have to keep stopping for the lighting blokes to fix the overheads. Once certain bits of the set, like the headers, are in position they can't bring the lighting bars down to re-focus them.'

We were sitting in the middle of the Coliseum canteen. This area is right under the stage and Brian told me that, pre-1974, the whole area housed the three huge motors which ran the Edwardian revolves[2] and was a mass of criss cross braces (to hold up the stage). It is now held up by the canteen pillars, which follow the lines of the three revolves. The original oak stage is still there, with its revolves, but it is overlaid by the modern stage – or rather by 84 sheets of hardboard that we replace every summer.

'Actually,' said Brian, 'I worked for the builders that refitted the Coliseum in '68. I was a chippie, all the planking in the PS and the Flys is mine. Cinerama (the previous owners) had taken out the central section of the Dress Circle for their projectors and just chucked it; it was solid marble, we have plasterwork in that bit now. Lots of things went then. George Midwinter (the Maintenance Manager) was wondering the other day what had happened to the original orchestra rails and I said, I can tell you exactly where they are, they're in the air duct under the first four rows of the Stalls; I remember them being thrown in.'

The Erda trap was above us in the canteen ceiling (Erda is, of course, the contralto who comes up from the ENO canteen to warn Wotan to Give Up the Ring in *Rhinegold*). Anne Collins was ENO's definitive Erda in the 70s and the sight of her trap produced a spate of fond memories – particularly her playing of the ghost of Antonia's mother from a fork lift truck in *Hoffmann*. From this it was short step to the inevitable touring stories. In Peterborough, Brian told me, he and the lads had celebrated the moon landing by mocking up a space rocket to replace the tiny balloon that used to zip across the sky in *Orpheus in the Underworld*.

'The audience loved it – but we nearly got sacked for that.'

And then came the really appalling tales, like the collapse of a hotel bar on top of Brian, some Wardrobe staff and three distinguished mezzo sopranos in Bristol. Fortunately he was summoned back on stage before he could carry on.

Notes

1 'Pros' is short for proscenium. Apart from the Coliseum's real proscenium arch (the outside edge of the stage) the stage sometimes acquires a 'show proscenium'. This is normally an extra header and two side flats. Further refinements can be found on page 166.

2 The Edwardian Coliseum was famous for its revolving stage.

19
The Sound Box

January 26th

Most of this show was spent in the Sound Box. I moved off there in the Interval, passing Amanda and some of the crew gathered round the Bridge. It was in pieces and they seemed to be trying to jam it together. It seemed an odd time to be testing it out.

The door to the Sound Box is just by the Stalls Bar and one slides in there past people deep in their Interval drinks. The box has detachable windows, so the technicians can hear exactly what is going on in the auditorium. These present something of a problem in performance as the audience, only a foot away, could feasibly hear every noise the technicians make, was it not for the fact that, by dint of long practice, they are extraordinarily stealthy in all their movements. A more serious disadvantage is that, although the Prompt Corner and other interested parties can talk to Sound through the walkie-talkie system, they can not answer back. Not, at least, at any length. In times of crisis therefore problems have to be sorted out by telepathy.

The Lighting Box next door is glazed and the guys there can clatter about as much as they like although one of them, Tom Mannings, told me there had been a famous night when the audience put in a complaint about the noise of champagne corks.

Emma was already in the box as I came in, writing memos; she told me that she or Julia were in every night, to keep an eye on the production and make the odd note. Julia normally bagged a seat in the Stalls, but Emma found the Sound Box more restful. There were never very many notes to give out for *Xerxes*.

'Everybody knows what they are doing,' she said, 'the most I have to do is tweak a couple of entrances. Actually, the principals are so experienced that they don't need notes – and I wouldn't dare give them one anyway.'

Lucy arrived at this moment, brushed me off her chair, established contact with Nicole in the Prompt Corner, and rolled the sound FX keyboard across the sound console. This ran on its own tracks, and looked like an ordinary keyboard of two octaves; however, it was linked up to a digital sampler (where the FX are stored) and pressing the appropriate key produced a sound effect. The first five keys were labelled Crash, Explosion, Crash and Rumble, Delayed Rumble and Rumble. In front of the keyboard were some slide volume controls; one said Lute, and the others Crash OP 1L/2R and Rumble OP 3L/4R.

The act started and Lucy's first cue came through, to enhance the sound of the lute. A cue light went on as Nicole spoke to Lucy over the headset; Lucy managed a whispered 'Stand by' and pushed the lute volume control up.

The box turned out to be rather a nice place to see the opera: the sound was good, there was plenty of room to draw and we were a head above the Stalls. Also one absolutely can't make polite conversation so there was no reason not to be absorbed in the stage.

As we came up to the Storm Scene Lucy took the sound cue sheet off its stand and studied it earnestly; then she ran her fingers over the keyboard.

'I always have to practise this,' she whispered.

My hair was standing on end. Of course she knew all the mikes and speakers were turned off but what confidence! And supposing they hadn't been . . .

The cues for the storm effects are not treated as visual cues though tonight it would probably have been better if they had been. Lucy got a cue for the first rumble on the right bar but Elviro came on late. His business got slower and slower and, towards the end of his recitative, I heard Lucy mutter, 'I'm running out of rumble.'

The rumble effect is produced by simply pressing the right key on the keyboard and playing with the slide volume control. She gave us a splendid explosion but the bridge did not break. Paul didn't seem to be too surprised but Lucy groaned with mortification as she went on to provide another rumble, which faded away just as the pillars flew in.

After the performance Lucy went through the various keys. They use a variety of speakers to give the impression of a thunderstorm going over.

'The first rumble,' she said, 'is on the first and second speakers backstage, the second rumble and explosion is on a third over the stage and the last rumble is on a fourth pointed at the dome. I don't suppose anybody notices.'

(Actually several people told me later that they had always sensed the storm moving overhead.)

She and Emma settled down to discuss why Paul had entered late. Emma thought there was a hold-up as the courtiers left the stage and that Paul had to wait for them. she promised to look into it.

I arrived PS for Act III to find Amanda standing by the extremely intact bridge.

'What happened?' I asked.

'Hah!' said Amanda. 'Somebody repaired it yesterday and left some solder in. Before the show we used a metal grinder to try and dislodge the solder, and all we got was some sparks. Then we tried again in the interval and got some very teeth-jarring noises. So we gave up and warned Paul that it wouldn't collapse.' (I noticed they didn't tell Lucy).

'There'll be some unhappy people around tomorrow morning,' she added grimly.

20
The Flys

February 2nd

In between shows I took a school party round as the crew re-set *Rosenkavalier* and, though I had to restrain the children's enthusiasm to climb right up to the Fly gallery, the very next performance of *Xerxes* found me on the phone to the Flys, to see if I could go up there myself.

Sure,' said a laid-back voice, 'No problem, just come up the spiral staircase and turn left over the bridge.'

The spiral staircase to the Flys is one of the original Edwardian fixtures and is situated just behind the back wall of the theatre on the OP side. It makes five complete turns before it gets to the top and has a very narrow tread; Paddy (one of the Flymen) told me later that it is the most ghastly thing to rush down if there's only five minutes left before closing time. At the top I found a deserted gallery on the OP side and, on my left, a bridge spanning the back wall. I looked

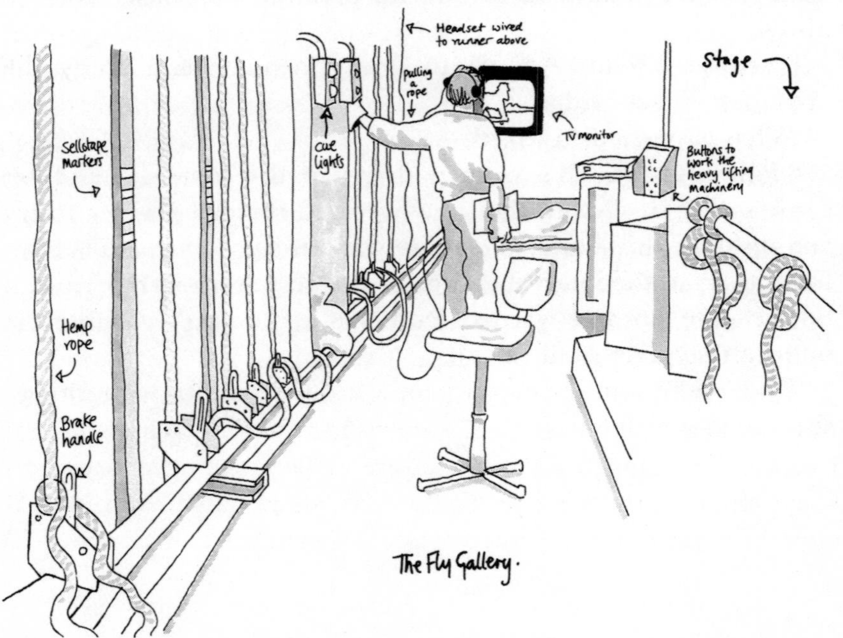

The Fly Gallery.

long and hard at that bridge: made of a couple of planks and, cradled in a V-shaped metal frame, it was so very like something from *Raiders of the Lost Ark* that I almost heard the cataract roaring beneath. However, a cautious couple of minutes later, I was over and a short Jacob's ladder brought me into the Fly Gallery itself.

The Gallery is also vintage 1904, wide, metal and sturdy, with a bench running along a rail on the right and the ropes strung along the wall on the left. Andy the Head Flyman was up there, reading at a little eyrie set up in the middle, but he courteously put the book aside to load me with technicalities.

Brian had already told me that ENO use a 2-in-1 system, that is, one foot of rope moves two feet of scenery, and though I could see nothing but hemp rope, Andy said that the scenery is actually flown on metal wire. The wire is attached to the rope that the Flymen pull. Wire, of course, would cut their hands to pieces.

The Flys are marked up for four shows at a time. Each show in the rep has a different colour: *Xerxes* is a white show, *Fledermaus* a red; the other colours are yellow and green. Every rope runs beside a vertical black bar which has four strips of coloured Sellotape stuck on it, corresponding to similar strips of Sellotape stuck round the rope at the top and bottom of its run. When the strips coincide the flown scenery is 'on its dead' – either properly up in the grid, or in place on the stage. Obviously for *Xerxes* the Flymen are only watching the white strips of Sellotape as the red *Fledermaus* strips would bring the cloths in at different levels. Intermediate levels are also marked if they are important; the Hedge Curtain in the Hedge Clipping Scene, for example, has to come in very precisely, masking the trolley on which Mike is standing, and showing only his head and shoulders. The mark on the rope for this cue is a special 'dead', a strip of white tape flanked by two bits of blue tape (to highlight it).

Everything in the Flys was geared for maximum visibility and for leaving the hands free: Andy's headset was wired up on a runner that zipped along the entire Gallery (he never seemed to get entangled), the cue lights were extra large; and the DS monitor (showing the stage picture) was the size of a normal TV.

Some other Flymen, Jamie and Paddy, clattered up and I asked them if there were any other ways up that didn't include the Zambezi bridge. Sure, said everyone and Andy pointed to a Jacob's ladder that went straight down the wall to the PS wing some 40 feet below.

'Its nice and quick if you want a beer,' said Paddy, who seems to descend to ground level for no other purpose.

The Overture started and they moved DS to pull up the Hedge Curtain; I noticed that the Flymen were in position long before they pulled. Jamie and another guy were on the rope, Paddy was on a stay rope and Andy watched the stage and the monitor. He was also listening for Nicole to give the cue through the headset. When they *did* pull I was amazed at the physical effort involved: from the top of their stretch, right down, the movement was so fast that it was difficult to believe they retained any control. Meanwhile Andy bellowed encouragingly at them:

Pulling a rope.

'Keep going, keep going, faster, faster! We're losing it! Get up there! – Oh great, very nice.'

I asked Jamie what the stay rope was for and he explained that, as the Hedge Curtain is extremely heavy, the diagonal rope gives them more purchase, a simple matter of pulley physics. The Hedge is counterweighted of course but it doesn't just hit the stage, its bottom actually sits on the stage (in graceful curves). This means that the counterweight loses some of its effect and they have to pull harder to get it up again. The diagonal rope gives them extra power.

Bringing in the Hedge for the Hedge Clipping scene was even more manic, Nicole's measured, 'Six, five, four, three . . . slow down . . . two, one, perfect!' translated into the three chaps hauling away like lunatics while Andy tried to interpret the countdown:

'Okay . . . No! Slow it!' he called, then, 'Speed it up, speed it up!' (It didn't seem to me they could go any faster.) There was a terrific flurry at the end.

'Tie it up!' cried Andy as the 'special dead' appeared and Paddy whipped the stay rope round the bar. I had to remember that their speed was half that of the curtain's.

After that there was a lull and the Gallery emptied. Andy said *Xerxes* was quite a busy show and the breaks in it were an irritating 10 minutes, which barely gave you time to go down to the canteen for tea. They have a little hidy-hole under the Jacob's ladder at the end of the bridge where they flake out. This has the added strategic advantage of enabling them to hear the footsteps of anybody who comes into the Flys. (I didn't discover this until I came over during Act II: 'Who's there?!' said a voice below me, just as I was negotiating the ladder; it was like being suddenly addressed by a troll.)

Paddy hung on to chat and to look over my drawing. I could see the rice bag hanging US and I asked him how difficult it was to operate.

'Oh, it's dead easy,' he said, 'But you can't control the flow. That all depends on how evenly the rice has been poured in. It's always steady at first and then it usually goes in streaks. I did the snow in *Christmas Eve*, that was a fiddly show and I got muddled as to whether the dead was in or out. At least with a flat you can see whether it's up or down, anyway I took a chance – and pulled the wrong rope. All the snow shot out the top of the bag. Four inches of the stuff fell in one second, some of the generals had great mounds of it, piled on their caps and epaulettes. Still, everybody said it looked nice.'

He told me that he had started off as a member of the stage crew but much preferred being in the Flys. There are far fewer of them up there, which clearly makes for a more democratic atmosphere.

'Here' he said, 'we talk things through and sort them out; there's less of a "Hey you!" mentality. The only real problem is we become invisible to the crew. They forget about us. For example, they will push the bottom of a flat to make way for something onstage. Of course, a flat comes in vertical and if you shove it, it goes up at an angle, swings about to right itself and clangs against all the other stuff in the Flys.'

In spite of these irritations, however, the Flys appeared to be a relaxed and friendly place and relatively independent of the power structures below. Jamie told me later that although there's really nowhere to go once you're a Flyman he couldn't bear the idea of giving it up.

Paddy said their shift was 8 a.m. to 11 p.m., later some nights, three days on, three days off. As the day is spent flying things in and out for rehearsals, lighting set-ups and change-overs, this must mean their time of maximum weariness is the show itself.

'How many people do you need to run a show?' I asked.

'You can't tell, some shows only need one. But then the *Nutcracker* last Christmas needed seventeen, and two huge TV screens, for all those transformation scenes. It was like a bloody pantomime up here.'

I asked him about flying people.

'The thing is, you have to fly them from the stage. If their first entrance is flown we send them up in their chariot, or whatever, before the show starts and they have to wait for their entrance up there. Of course, if they go up in the middle of an act they'll have to stay up, till the Interval, before we can get them down.'

However, they made an exception for *Gianni Schicchi*. In this opera an actor played the (deceased) eponymous hero and flew off to Heaven, in a cradle, at the start of the show. The opera has no interval so, rather leave him up there, they pulled up the cradle until it was parallel with the gate in the bridge, swung it over and got him out.

'Though one day we all went off for tea and left him stranded. We'd just forgotten. The actor went completely mental. He swung the cradle to and fro until it reached the bridge, grabbed the gate and pulled himself out. Then he turned up in the canteen to tell us what he thought of us.'

He left me to get on with my drawing and I found myself the sole occupant of the Flys for the Library Scene. It is a nice place from which to see a show, in fact, in a boxed set like *Xerxes*, you actually see more of the action up there than from the wings. And the sound is excellent.

I stayed in the Gallery until the Storm Scene during which Andy kept an eye on the cue light while Paddy joggled the rice out. The thunder up there sounded particularly terrible and I noticed that they only needed one man, Jamie, on the rope for the Pillars.

I went back across the plank bridge much easier in mind, only to find the spiral staircase more difficult to negotiate going down than coming up. Not even the prospect of missing Closing Time would have induced me to go faster.

Joggling the rain bag

21
Covers

February 9th and 11th

Meanwhile, back on Earth, sickness was stalking the company. Louise Winter had recovered from her illness but, in the week's break between the fifth and sixth performances, Yvonne Kenny and Chris Robson had gone down with throat infections. Their covers (Sally Harris and Andrew Watts) went on on the 9th, but I was off too and didn't see them. The next performance night Charles Kraus, the Company Manager , told me we were halfway back to normal.

'Yvonne's back, thank goodness, but Chris is still unwell and we haven't got a cover. This would be the one night Andrew is N/A[1], the only other singer who knows the part is in Ireland.'

Sally Harris was down in the canteen and told me what it had been like to go on as Romilda.

'I knew it was a possibility last Monday' she said, 'and on the day I did feel rather shaky but I got over that once I came in. When I *did* get worried was at the call for Beginners. But before I knew it, I was on. The most alarming part was when the back wall doors opened and I saw *all* the Chorus looking at me. We'd never rehearsed with the Chorus. After that I enjoyed it. It was a great help having Andrew on as well, after all we'd been rehearsing together in cover rehearsals.'

Up in the wing I found Amanda putting out a call for a PS electrician to come and set a music stand; Lucy was fiddling around with the mike connections for a stage announcement and a young man was singing one of Arsamenes' arias to the empty House. Jean passed me on her way to the Box Office and told me that Chris had come in to walk the part (that is, go through the motions of the role while remaining mute) while Nicholas Clapton was going to sing it from the PS run-out.

'He's been learning it all day,' she said. 'I hope Yvonne's feeling all right. You have to tell the Company Office by 11 o'clock whether you're okay for the evening. But how can you tell that early?'

On stage Catherine Garland, one of the stage recorder players was practising the sopranino line.

'Hi,' she said. 'We've only got one recorder tonight. The treble's off.'

'Don't they want you to play the treble?'

'Apparently not. We play in unison anyway, and Ivor thinks the sopranino is more audible.'

Any ideas I was beginning to harbour that this was the Doomed Show were put to rest by the appearance of the principals; Chris Robson was clearly getting ready to enjoy himself, Yvonne sailed into the wing looking particularly cheerful and Louise landed me a massive slosh on the back and told me I shouldn't be drawing in the dark. Nicholas Clapton, in black trousers and jumper, disappeared out front and the House Manager went in front of the Curtain to explain to the audience the peculiar nature of this evening's performance.

Actually, they look better...
Drawing in the dark.

The opera went like a breeze. Friends out front said that Chris, released from vast portions of the score, was having a wonderful time. 'He's rather like a silent movie,' said one of them. He sang the recitative, and a couple of the smaller arias, but let Nicholas do the rest – though whenever his substitute took over he couldn't resist doing a double act. Nicholas's top notes got some particularly encouraging looks; the audience loved it. Some parts of the opera suddenly struck people as very funny, particularly Romilda's, '*I'm speechless!*', in fact the whole show went with a swing.

I watched parts of the show from a crack in the OP scenery and even from this limited viewpoint it was obvious that the cast were going for detail. Louise took for ever to choose her cake in the Coffee House Scene, (to the manifest discomfort of the Warden); Mike (from the top of his hedge) regarded Arsamenes, Elviro *and* Nicholas with steady disapproval; and, on a quieter note, Yvonne wiped away a genuine tear during '*That ruthless Tyrant*'.

Indeed by the time we got to the *sinfonia* in Act III everybody on stage was enjoying themselves so much that even Mike began to crack. Mark won the bowls game by actually hitting the jack (a first) and he raised his fist in triumph as he left the stage.

However, while this was going on out front, backstage the show was dominated by the Rice Skid Patch. Some of the rice from the storm scene had spilled on to the OP planking at the back – just out of reach of a stage broom – and every principal found themselves slipping on it as they came round the US OP corner. Nerys did a wonderful slide into the wing after her despairing, '*No, no, though you detest me*', Louise nearly crashed on her furious exit ('*I'll make you the widow of those kisses*') and we still had the Quarrel Duet to go.

Just before she went on for this, Yvonne had said dubiously, 'I'm about to have a quarrel with somebody who isn't there.' So far Chris had not mimed the words he didn't sing and Nicholas's disembodied voice carrying on what is, after all, a pretty snappy dialogue from the other side of the stage must have been extremely disconcerting. However, at the start of the duet Chris began to sing his part in a *pianissimo* baritone and by the middle section the piece was going famously. Both the principals came pounding off for the run-around, up to the OP corner . . . and straight into the rice. Yvonne slithered into the wing, said something in Australian, and dashed on; Chris, less luckily, crashed into the Winged God, fell over a ramp – and *still* made it to the stage on the beat.

He and Nick sang in the final chorus by which time the high spirits on stage had begun to affect the props. One bust was feeling very cheerful, refusing to get broken in '*Rise Ye Furies*,' and, while its mates were being swept up, rolled down to the front of the stage for the curtain calls.

Notes

1 N/A is Not Available. Singers negotiate their availability for performances and rehearsals at the contract stage.

22
Rosenkavalier

Towards the end of the run *Rosenkavalier* joined the rep. We had all been so conscious of this immense show, rehearsing parallel to *Xerxes* and (to tell the truth) rather getting in our way backstage, that I decided to take a night off and watch it from the wings.

Coming into the OP, just before the Overture, I found Amanda sitting at the prompt desk in a deserted wing.

'Where *is* everybody?' I asked.

'Oh, this is a very quiet Act,' she replied.

She leafed through the Book. It seemed almost blank.

'What do you do?' I asked.

'Very little really. In Act I, I ring the bell for the Marschellin's chocolate.'

She indicated a little handbell on the prompt desk and, with that to look forward to, I dodged behind some lamps to watch the show.

To my amazement (after the boxed-in *Xerxes*) the whole downstage area was clearly visible. I could see the raked, highly polished floor clearly, and was not surprised to find the whole cast resorting to the rosin tray before they ventured on.

One of the footman smothered his shoes in the stuff. 'It's really slippery out there,' he said, '*and* I'm carrying a tray. I've nearly gone over twice.'

The little boy playing Muhammed was just as thorough, burdened as he is with the Marschallin's breakfast. Even Octavian rosined her stockinged feet.

However, once they were all on, the stillness in the wing became positively eerie. Amanda sat in the Prompt Corner peacefully turning the pages of the score, and nothing ever seemed to happen. Our only visitors were the other Muhammeds (the covers and the children who take over in Acts II and III). They came up to inspect their colleague as he poured hot chocolate, and disappeared the moment he exited. It seemed a rather specalised view of *Rosenkavalier*.

However, the two shows were not dissimilar. Like *Xerxes*, *Rosenkavalier* boasts a variety of weather, including real water for rain. I was just admiring the pierced hosepipe that creates the effect when the whole contraption was upstaged by a genuine thunderstorm. Rain thundered on the glass roof, window panes clanged in the wind and the ASM, Alex Hayesmore, moved swiftly US to find a mop.

'Terrible racket isn't it?' said Amanda. 'It sounds worse on stage, and they have to sing over it.'

'Can the audience hear it?'

'Oh yes, but not so bad.'

The storm blew over and, as the Marschallin reflected on the passing of time, I decided that the Act was going to end in the monastic calm with which it began. I was wrong. The *Rosenkavalier* sets are some of the heaviest in the current repertory and the change-over between Acts is frantic. As the Rose was handed over to Muhammed the wing began to fill up with stage crew; somebody turned the side TV monitors off and an anticipatory buzz was shushed by the Stage Manager (Anita White). The Marschellin lit her melancholy cigarette while a couple of chaps were already reaching for some ropes and the moment the curtain came down the place went berserk.

Anita swept back the blacks, a prop bloke ran past me with pillows, the slide lights were swung out of the way and huge black flats were already flapping over our heads as the Marschellin walked composedly down the wing to her dressing room.

After 20 hectic minutes Act II was set and I resurfaced in the PS. I was alone again – apart from a mysterious furry shape in the dog-seller's basket and

Murray conducting the Off stage band.

the Silver Rose itself. Seeing it was just sitting on the prop tray I assumed it was *not* silver after all.' Nor, presumably, did it have a drop of attar of roses on its petals. However, I didn't check.

The chorus started off in the OP to sing the greeting to Octavian, '*Rofrano! Rofrano!*' and exited PS after the presentation of the Rose. By the middle of the Act it was getting rather a tight fit and, as always, I was amazed to see how much noise a company can make and *still* not be heard out in front.[2] Alex sat tranquilly amongst the row, cueing in Faninal and Ochs, and urging the chorus to shout louder when the latter's retinue ran amok.

I was still in the PS at the beginning of Act III when a member of the offstage band wandered up from the pit.

'Hi,' she said, 'I'm the mobile cello.'

She disappeared US, reminding me that Lucy had said an epic took place OP US in this Act. And, lo, when I walked round the back of the scenery I found a 22-piece band (complete with piano) crammed in amongst the golden statues. These are the offstage musicians to whom Ochs takes such an exception and are usually represented on stage by a couple of gypsy fiddlers. Murray Hipkin was conducting them, linked to the Pit via headphones and TV monitor (though he was actually *leading* the band).

The Sound Department, Colin and Christine were very much in evidence, guarding their mikes and trying to ensure the one in front of Murray didn't get swept away by his conducting. I stood listening to the music with Colin who was charmed to find I had drawn him; he reappeared in the wing three minutes later in a bow tie.

He and Christine watched the band like hawks, ready to spring into action and remove the mikes the moment the band finished.

'Is it always this split second?' I asked.

Snappy dressing in the Sound Department

'No, of course we *could* do it easier,' said Colin, 'we just like to create crises'.

Meanwhile life was hotting up in the Prompt Corner. On stage Octavian's practical joke was in full swing and apparitions were popping out of trap doors and windows to the accompaniment of ghostly spotlights. Amanda said it was her favourite moment in Act III and for five minutes everybody got a steady stream of crisp directions.

'Stand by LX 5. Go, LX 5. Stand by with the trap. Go, trap.' and so on.

At the very end of the opera I slipped out of the corner and joined the crowd listening to the Trio. From where we stood (the first downstage entrance in the OP) the huge amber lights opposite shone right into our eyes. None of us could see the stage and the singers appeared suffused in a curious golden haze. They sounded wonderful. I am not sure we were not standing in the best place in the house.

Notes

1 It is different down the road. The ROH rose really is silver and was originally given them by the family of Hugo von Hofmannsthal. Just before a performance of *Rosenkavalier* the House Manager takes it from the display safe and delivers it to the Stage Manager. From then on it is always in the eyeline of somebody and is removed from the singers the moment they exit. The House Manager reappears at the end of Act II to put it back in the safe.

2 I was assured that the heavy sets absorbed most of the sound.

23
The Lighting Rig and a Crash

February 14th

Three inches of snow fell in the night and everybody turned up at the theatre in varieties of snow-gear.

I went up on to the stage and found a girl from props tweaking the Tree. 'The whole point about this tree,' she said grimly, 'is that it's supposed to be a prize tree and instead it looks half-dead. It went wrong in the refit when it got the wrong leaves.'

I fingered them. They seemed to be made of stiffened cloth.

'They were made of linen this time round,' she said, 'and they go limp immediately.'

Charly Caruana was standing in the OP with Neville and I asked them how the Lighting Department managed to remember all the numbers of the lamps. Neville immediately started to expand on our wonderful circuitry,

'Of course, Charles Bristow set up all the circuits,' he said.

'Ah . . .' said the other guy appreciatively.

'Now, he was a Sadler's Wells man. Ah, that was the time to learn,' continued Neville and exited, which left us more or less where we started. Charly tried to explain the beauty of the system and, though I grasped that our circuits followed a splendid numerical order round the stage, their other excellences proved too much for me (but see page 162). We went round to the OP office afterwards to look at the circuit map: And then on to the dimmer room where the numbers reappeared as fuses, coloured according to their amps. I began to see that one would eventually remember that 197 (for example) was an OP lamp.

The major lighting effect in *Xerxes* is the weather on the cyclorama. We use five slides for the various skyscapes, projected from the PS side, and as the projector beam hits the cyc at an angle, the images on the slides have to be slightly distorted to compensate.

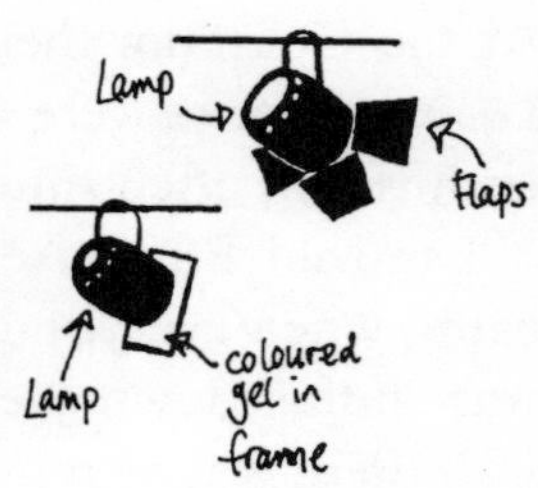

'We fade the slides in and out during the performance,' said Charly. 'You can bring one in as you're fading one out, but you can't *swap* the slides until the Interval. The projector shakes however careful you are.'

I asked him about the light spills.

'Yes, well they can be caused by anything. Wonky scenery. Badly hung blacks. Sometimes a lamp itself gets buckled, particularly the flaps. If we can get at them we wrap them up in black silver foil. Otherwise the guy on the Board has to work out which lamp is causing the spill and kill it.'

I said I was due to visit the Lighting Box before the next show.

'You ought to go up to the Limes Box as well. And the Grid.'

We both looked up.

'The floor up there is made of three-inch slats with three-inch holes in between,' he said. 'You have to watch where you are going, though. Especially,' he said as an afterthought, 'as there are bigger holes every now and then. Actually, there's another route to the Flys from here, up the ladders by the Prompt Corner and across the bridge behind the Proscenium. Mind you I always get lost.'

Much later, in Act II, there was a minor light spill during the Storm Scene. I noticed that Nicole immediately got on to the Board ('What's that horrible light on the wall?') and didn't write anything down on the Show Report until she could add 'killed by the Board.'

The Show Report is typed up by the Stage Manager after every show. It gives the exact timings of the opera, notes the replacements and lists any untoward events (with a view to making sure they never happen again). See illustration 17 for an example of one, and illustration 18 for an example of a show watch report.).

At the Coliseum they can be a minor art-form. The Copley *Don Giovanni* series were always a good read,[1] and the Stage Manager's enthusiasm often spills over into the write-up.

I moved PS as Act I started and, at the period of maximum calm, when everybody was lolling about on deckchairs and Chris was sliding down the OP wall singing '*When grief and pain assail me*', there was a tremendous crash.

Everybody on stage sprung to their feet and rushed into the OP wing while my first thought, I'm afraid, was 'Well at least I didn't do it . . . Two minutes later one of the crew, John Singh, ambled up.

'Where did that sound seem to come from, do you know?'

'US OP,' I said promptly.

'Hmm,' he said, 'we can't find it.'

I could scarcely believe that that amount of noise hadn't left a clearly visible trail of devastation; however, all the technicians in the PS were completely baffled. Chris (he whose aria had been ruined) passed laughing.

'What was it?' he said, 'a body falling from the flies?'

'It sounded like a lamp falling,' said John.

I went out front in the Interval to meet my sister.

'Did you hear a sort of crash?' I asked her.

'We *all* heard a crash. The whole audience jumped in their seats. What was it?'

'Nobody seems to know, where do *you* think it came from?'

Jane said that it was the considered opinion of her patch of the Stalls that it came from US Centre and that she thought it sounded like some stacked scenery behind the set falling over. 'If you want a layman's view" she added.

(The only person who had seemed unaffected by the noise, was she said, Chris. 'He just sort of flickered.')

After this I was scarcely surprised when Nick told me that the crash had been caused by some stacked *Rosenkavalier* 'gates' falling over upstage, centre. Jane Randall had been the first to rush US when the noise had happened but, as none of the *Xerxes* crew were involved, her eventual write-up of the incident (in the Show Report) was very laid-back: 'Act 1 Fly Q 4 The hedge caught the pelmet on the way in. It was quickly freed. There was a loud crash during Act 1 Sc 4, some gates falling over USC.

At the end of the Interval Amanda asked me what I'd heard about the crash.

'Apparently, it was the gates in the *Rosenkavalier* rostra,' I said carefully.

She laughed, 'You do sound professional' she said, and returned to slicing cake.

Shortly afterwards the PS had forgotten the whole incident in the excitement of a cake fight – I don't know who'd won, but it was quite obvious who'd lost.

As Act 3 got ready to start, the audience had a collective failure of nerve and went completely silent. A Warden came out to adjust some ropes, Ivor wasn't due in the Pit for another three minutes and Mike, the Warden who starts the Act, stood on guard in front of the Hedge Curtain, meditating in the quiet – his gloom deepening with every minute that passed.

Nicole was watching the scene on her TV monitor and dying of embarrassment, 'I hate it when they do this, look at them,' she said, 'why can't they talk to each other?'

Given the hiatus, it was a pity that this had to be the only night one of the performers missed a call. The curtain was held, Ivor was detained in the Prompt Corner and Nicole's calls for the defaulter moved from 'Your call, please, who-ever-it-was' to an anxious 'Will so-and-so please come to the stage?' Bob was just preparing to dash off to the dressing room when the absentee an on with an ingenuous, 'I'm sorry I was chattting!' and threw themselves into a deckchair.

Bob was very unfazed. 'Well, at least that's honest.' he said.

At the end of the show Jane Randall

began to pull back the blacks for the Quarrel run and, passing the portable TV stand where I was drawing, called Nicole over.

'Hi,' she said. 'Look at this silhouette of me and Bob.'

Nicole instantly leafed through the sketch pad. I'd already noticed that the longer patches of the score made her restive. In Act II, as Xerxes sang '*The heart that love has captured*', Yvonne had been leaning thoughtfully against the prompt desk.

'This is a huge aria,' she said.

Nicole agreed, 'Six minutes 33 seconds,' she'd said dolefully.

During the Finale she pointed out the agitated 'Blues off!' cue in the Bible.

'What are they?' I whispered.

'The show Light Blues,' she explained and, to make this clearer, switched them off and on as the singers went on for the first curtain call but as I couldn't see that anything had changed I was no further forward.[2]

The next thing we knew the cast were in the wings, listening to the roars of approval out front and very pleased with the show.

'That was a good one,' said Ivor.

'I'm enjoying them more and more,' said Louise.

They all crowded off stage together as Nicole turned the Blues off again and ahead of us, in the darkness, we heard a well-known lyric soprano. 'Hi! Who turned the lights off? We're going to break a leg.'

Nicole hastily switched the Blues *on* and they all swept cheerfully off, down to the dressing room corridor.

Notes

1 John Copley, a distinguished director much associated with English National Opera in the late 1970s.

2 I discoverd later that the Blues are the working lights used during a show; they are covered with a deep blue gel and go on when the real working lights are switched off. *I* found the light they cast was virtually undetectable; however, everybody else on stage considered them to be a tremendous help.

24

Lighting

The LX department seemed to be everywhere in the next couple of days.

I bumped into Tom Mannings (Electrics Supervisor) while reconnoitring a tour for a group of schoolchildren. He took my request (to invade the LX Box) with extraordinary calm.

'I bet you want me to go through Lighting in two minutes so you can pass it on,' he said. How right he was.

We went into the Lighting Box and stood by a desk that looked out over the Stalls.

'Well, as you know, all the lamps are numbered, so to bring them up you just punch in their number here.' He indicated a little keyboard embedded in the desk.

'Now, 305, for example, I know that's a lamp at the back of the stage. It's red at the moment. Watch this,' and, as he punched in 305, a red light appeared US, facing us directly.

'You can bring it up or fade it with this control,' he said, rolling a knob that looked like a volume control. The lamp brightened and faded as he did so and some Kirov dancers, practising on stage at that moment, looked about them nervously.

'So what we do is set up the stage and bring up all sorts of lamps, set their levels and play around until we've got a pretty picture, and then we enter the whole lot in the computer as one cue. You can punch in how long it should take and you can do all sorts of other things too, like punching in one cue to come in under another. So while one cue is fading out another is coming in.'

The children and I were deeply into this ten minutes later and were delighted to hear Tom say, 'Go on, punch in 305. Okay, now bring it up. And fade. Easy, isn't it?'

I discovered later that the business of *activating* each light cue was deceptively easy; the technician simply presses a lone button,

no matter how complicated the configuration of lamps. Lucy Paget (who started off in lighting) said that she used to study navigation in the LX Box, with charts spread all over the lighting desk. 'The button was just under Gravesend.'

However, if a cue has to be skipped or if anything goes wrong, the technician has to know not only how to override it but how to get into the computer, re-jig some cues, kill others and all sorts of complications, performed, of course, at high speed. The most bizarre accidents happen. In *The Two Widows*, for example, some chap caught a switch in his trouser turn-up and managed to turn off most of the lamps; fortunately the follow spots stayed on while they sorted out the others. (It took about 10secs).

Lucy gave me a print out of the *Xerxes* cue sheet for Lighting which, even with the information gained so far, remained a fairly baffling document. You will find it on p. 208.

Marian Staal, another Electrics Supervisor (there are three of them), took me through the hieroglyphics.

XF is a 'Cross Fade,' the change-over from one lighting cue to another; and MF, 'Move Fade', is a cue that involves some of the lamps changing *within* a lighting that is already set up (a person on stage might switch a light on, for example, or the cue might involve the changing light of clouds or mist). All the MFs in *Xerxes* are directly related to the weather.

O/L means the Opening Light – in this case already preset by the LX in the Interval – and 'Vis' halfway down the page indicates the cue is visual; that is, the technician will be *cued* by the Prompt Corner, but will do the cue in his own time as he watches the stage.(At the opening of Act III he has to wait for two thirds of the Hedge Curtain to fly out before he punches the button.) As the EOA (End of the Act) approaches he has to get ready for a 'DBO'. A DBO is a Dead Black Out, where everything is darkened, as opposed to a 'BO', an ordinary Black Out that might only be sectional.

In fact the LX abbreviate everything. Over on the right of the cue sheet, for example, you will find the length of time *between* cues listed and, amongst the numbers, are the letters TFP; they flag a particularly lengthy pause and mean Time For a Pint (usually a harmless cup of tea . . .)[1]

Talking to Marian later I discovered that although the Coliseum lighting rig is modern, the department's way of working is rather dated. Apart from the computer practically everything else to do with the lamps is manual.

'We've never got away from the idea,' she said, 'that a man is *on* a lamp, that we change the gels or alter the focus by hand. Mind you, our set-up forces us to be ingenious. One of our problems is that we have no really adequate way of lighting DS centre. Our first lighting bar is way too far back.[2] (See illustration 21) I was brooding about this up in the OP gallery the other day and realised that if I put in a bit of scaffolding up there I could get a very nice angle on the DS.'

She did so immediately – erecting scaffolding being, apparently, just one of her skills.

Ah Marion must
have found another
place for a lamp...

At the Coliseum we have a couple of hundred lamps in permanent positions in the rig (they are, of course, permanently focused) and others to hand should a show need them. (*Flying Dutchman*, for example, had about 80 per cent extra lighting since the designer wanted strong horizontal beams to come from the wings.) Like the other Electricians, Marian could tell you the number and position of practically any lamp in the rig and (like Charley dilating on the beauty of our circuitry) she too appeared to have an affinity for the lamps.

'When you get the focusing right,' she said, 'you can feel it, it's a physical sensation. It's a marvellous thing to set up a show. You recreate it from scratch during the afternoon change over. As I refocus I'm thinking, How did I set the lamp last time, did I get it right? You *modify* all the time. In the Lighting Box you hold the show in your hands.'

'So it's not just a question of hitting the button?'

'Oh no, the Board operator is the second pair of eyes. We may sometimes see the show better than the Stage Manager, in fact, we are the last people to look at the show before the audience come in. We run our checks right up to the in-coming. Lighting doesn't just happen in spite of the computer cues – lamps get knocked, the light spills – and the Board often crashes. We're there constantly, reacting to what is going on.'

I had picked up this intense interest in the job from so many of the people backstage that I was in danger of forgetting what it meant in practical terms. The hours worked by the LX Show Managers brought me down to earth.[3]

'We have no maximum hours,' she said, 'and just before a new opera it is quite common for the Show Managers to be in from 8 a.m. in the morning right through to 11 p.m. the *next* evening, with no sleep in between.' she said. 'It is lucky we've got a passion for the job . . .'

Notes

1 This habit has the advantage of obscuring breezy comments on other people's problems – NFI, for example, is usually translated 'Not F****** Interested'.

2 The LX have designated bars in the Flys from which they sling their lamps. There are 71 bars up in the Flys, with number 1 starting just behind the Proscenium arch. The first LX bar is number 10.

3 These long sessions are not of course *unique* to the Show Managers. Many Coliseum departments find themselves working equally long hours.

25
The Performers

February 16th

I settled down with a sketch book at 6.30 and found that Phil, one of the firemen, had already been summoned to bring in the Iron. He stood downstage as firemen do in the PS, smiling genially at the work going on around him, and one of the LX chaps said to me, 'If you want to do a still life you should do him . . .'

Phil was quite unruffled, 'I'm still,' he said, 'because I'm a nocturnal creature.'

I asked him how the Iron was released.

'I just push a button and pull a lever,' he said, disappearing into a couple of black drapes; scraps of information filtered through the material. 'The lever releases the brake; the Iron weighs 11 tons and it has to come down in 30 seconds. Legally we should be able to pull it up manually, if we have to, just using two blokes. I've never seen it done.'

Brian told me later that the Iron had once been worked by a hydraulic system which had made everybody acutely aware of the current state of the London water gauge; if the water pressure went down, down came the Iron no matter what was going on. One night it calmly obliterated a Gala in front of HM the Queen Mother and some luckless tech had to winch it up again at 15 turns an inch.

'Mind you, it was worse at Sadlers Wells. There the last guy in of a morning had to winch up the Iron *every day*.'

Amanda started to pull blacks along the rail, obscuring my view, so I took a chair US and drew a comprehensive picture from there of the whole wing. Two crew men, Nick and Carl, were on the back wall that evening and, having removed the 25kg weights from its back supports (so it could be flown after the Concert

Scene) came over to watch my progress. Carl took the picture very seriously and got impatient with Nick who beguiled the time by dredging up unlikely technical terms that I might find interesting.

From him I learnt that *Xerxes* merely has a Show Proscenium (ie it is part of the set) and that a proper *False* Proscenium (made for a specific show) is a black border with its top and sides all of a piece. A False Proscenium in which the header and the sides are separate is really just a Teaser with two Tormentors. While I was digesting this, he added that a Monkey Stick was a rod on a line that helped you throw a cleat. At this point my bewilderment must have been patent. 'They're only used for very tall flats,' he explained.

I chewed this over as I watched the crew assemble the set on the Last Night of the opera. The cleats, I realised were like the flanges you get on flagpoles to secure the rope. They attach the flats horizontally to the surrounding scenery and stop them flapping about when the doors are opened and closed. Nobody seemed to need a Monkey Stick and the flick of the wrist with which the techs achieved it looked jolly easy but presumably took years of practice.

Nick mooched off DS, eventually sitting in front of the Handel statue, uncannily mirroring its pose. I drew him into the foreground. Carl was extremely indignant. 'What's he doing there?' he said. 'You need to put in some more creases. His Derby's twice as big as that.'

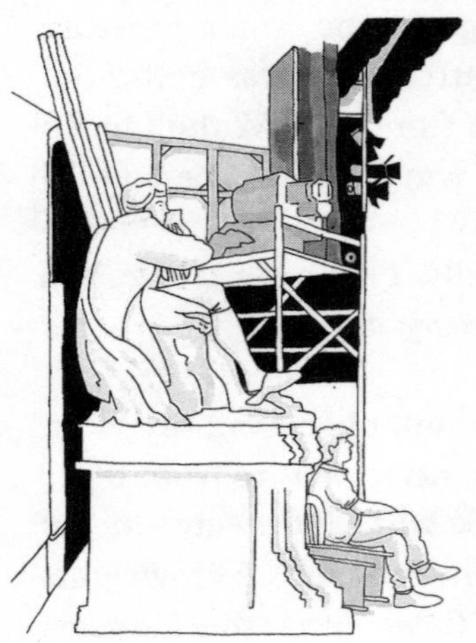

Nick passed us later, ostentatiously holding his tummy in.

I went on drawing, idly watching singers go back and forth. They all seemed to be commenting on each other's performances tonight. Louise passed Yvonne after '*No stain can blemish*'. 'It sounds wonderful,' she said.

'Does it?' said Yvonne. 'Bless you!' And they went off clicking their fingers to the *ritornello* of Jean's next aria.

Everybody seemed to be in terrific spirits but then *Xerxes* is famous for being a happy show. Ann Murray said that she remembered spending the whole of the first run laughing. 'Nick [Hytner] had a talent for letting people laugh. I loved that show from beginning to end. It was fun just *being* there.'

Nerys would have endorsed this; she sat down to say how much she was enjoying herself and what a wonderful producer Hytner was.'

'Something Nick Hytner said to me in rehearsal made a huge difference. He said, "Don't try and make the audience like you. Just work on the character, take them into your confidence and they *will* like you." Of course, I want the whole audience to love me! But I've come to see that if I just get on with the character, the effect will take care of itself.'

Chris Robson meanwhile was getting on with it and bringing people to a standstill, first with a burst of extempore ornamentations, and next by sending Elviro about his business with some furious (and unscripted) 'Hahs!'

'*What* was he doing in Munich yesterday?' said Paul as he came off stage.[1]

During the Interval some friends out front told me that the Wardens were also putting on an extraordinary show and I got back to find them clustered round the cake trolley. The orchestra were tuning up and suddenly all six of them raised their trays and sang a broken chord.

'It's called tray tuning,' said Mark.

Amanda groaned, 'The trouble is,' she said (once they were all safely on stage), 'that there is an ex-Warden in the audience and they're all playing to him like mad.'

A girl from Wigs asked how the Wardens would be dressed in other productions and it took us some trouble to convince her that they only existed in this production because of the Egg, the cactuses, coffee cups and so on. The Handel Opera Society had put on *Xerxes* with four 'supers' (indeed, I don't know the Handel Opera that actually needs more).

I went back to the PS to finish the Handel statue as Carl frowned over my shoulder.

'If they ever dead this show,' he said, 'that's the prop I would like.' (The Handel statue is about a third bigger than the V&A original.)

'Wouldn't it be rather in the way in a flat?' I said.

'Not at all, I'd cut out the front and stick a fridge in there.'

On stage meanwhile Ash Wednesday had struck: there was no chocolate cake on the trolley. Louise was thunderstruck. 'Where's the chocolate one?' she said in a Stage Whisper (Row F got it nicely) to the hapless Warden. The others came off delighted.

The rainbow aria ('*Those loves cross'd by fortune*') ended a brilliant Act II. One of the chorus ladies said as they exited, 'That must be the most wonderful aria in the piece.'

'Yes, Romilda's come through hasn't she?' said Yvonne.

I looked through Amanda's Running Sheets at the beginning of Act III and told her how stage management language was beginning to permeate my ordinary life, she sighed, 'Oh, me too. I say 'Ready and . . . Go' even when I'm helping in the kitchen'

It's frightfully unnerving talking to Amanda, especially as Elviro's fast exit gets nearer, since she always appears to be giving you her full attention although the headset chat must be absorbed subconsciously. Paul, the door operator, came over to talk and I kept a nervous eye on the DS cue light. As it went red, he slowly began to move back. Amanda said warningly, 'Paul, this is a fast cue,' but he seemed in a daze.

'Paul, it's fast.' The light went green and still he hovered.

'Now, Paul,' and he opened the door just before Elviro broke his nose on it. Paul and Amanda returned to our conversation as if nothing had happened.

Back on stage Chris was in a fine frenzy: he'd spat so closely to Louise in '*Yes, I want her*' that somebody from the Stalls had audibly wondered if it was supposed to be germ warfare, and now he was chucking the deckchairs around with such enthusiasm that one of the Wardens had to re-assemble his before he could carry it off.

Louise came up behind me just before the Bowls Scene, to peer at the sketch pad. 'You can't see a thing!' she said, 'Does it look better like that?'

The Bowls Scene itself was enlivened by Mark deciding the jack hadn't been thrown far enough. So he kicked it further as he crossed the stage. The other Generals shook their fists at him.

Jean gave a heart-rending account of '*I am the cause of my own ruin*', and as she came off I said, 'That was wonderful.'

Jean stopped, 'It says it all,' she said simply, 'she knows she loves him too much.' Then, more pragmatically, 'Actually I had a frog in my throat. Amanda said that she could tell I was really feeling the emotion . . . I didn't like to tell her why.'

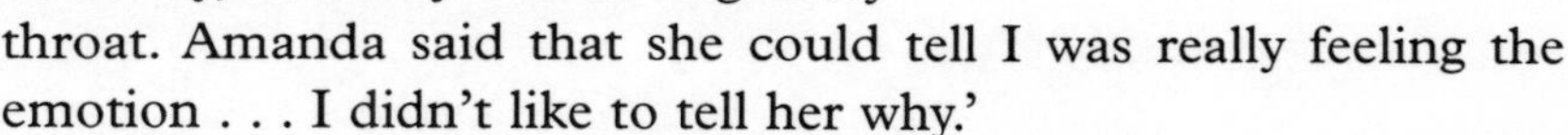

On stage Louise was just starting '*Rise ye furies*' and Jean paused to mime the words. 'I've always wanted to sing that,' she said, 'I've got the notes but I couldn't sing it in that key.' At this moment Louise launched into the high runs. 'Yes, well, it *is* very difficult.'

The curtain calls were enlivened by Chris and Nerys imitating Yvonne's cadenzas in '*Dearest and best of lovers*', 'I've never heard that sung so well,' said Chris, and I left thinking that everybody's performances had reached their absolute zenith. Inevitably Jean brought me swiftly down to earth.

'Could you come and draw some stories for Daniel's [her eldest son] birthday?' she asked me as we left the stage.

'Sure,' I said, 'what sort of stories does he like?'

'Oh, Ninja turtles. And Batman. They all rush around with towels tucked into the necks of their pyjamas . . .'

Note

1 During the *Xerxes* run Christopher Robson was commuting to Munich as he rehearsed Tolomeo in Richard Jones's production of *Giulio Cesare*.

26
The Last Night

I took a friend up on stage and bumped into Brian.

'Hallo!' he said with his ready tact, 'Where's the book, then? I wanted a signed copy tonight.'

'Oh *that* book,' said Amanda. 'It's cost us a fortune to get her to give us a good write-up.'

At 6.15 I was due at the Wig Room to see the Wardens having their bald caps fitted. The caps are a *Xerxes* speciality, indeed, when the show goes on tour somebody from Wigs usually has to travel over with it, to teach the make up staff abroad how to fit them (many foreign houses don't actually have a Wig Department).

The Wig Room was crowded: mirrors, swivel chairs, actors, Make up people and heads of hair. There was a Last Night buzz in the air, typified by Keziah, who was sporting a Romilda wig from the last run plus a pair of appalling eye lashes.

The Wardens turned up, in their breeches and shirt stage, and were immediately enveloped in an overall and put in front of a mirror. One of the girls slicked down their hair (very flat) and pulled a muslin cap over each head which she rapidly shaped, round the ears and the nape of the neck, by trimming its edge with a pair of scissors. The cap ends up with a couple of flaps in front of the ears and a long flap down the back of the neck. The whole thing was smoothed down, to remove any wrinkles from the hair underneath, and the ear flaps glued to the face (the Warden usually ended up holding these until they've stuck); the nape of the neck, I noticed, took a lot of smoothing down but, once this had stuck properly, the Warden was handed over to Keziah, to have white stuff slapped all over the top of his head.

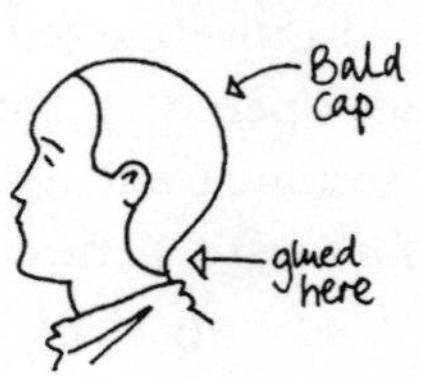

Once that was done he moved on to Rachel who covered the face, very thoroughly. The paste went everywhere – neck, eyelids, outer part of the ear – creating a mask-like effect which was

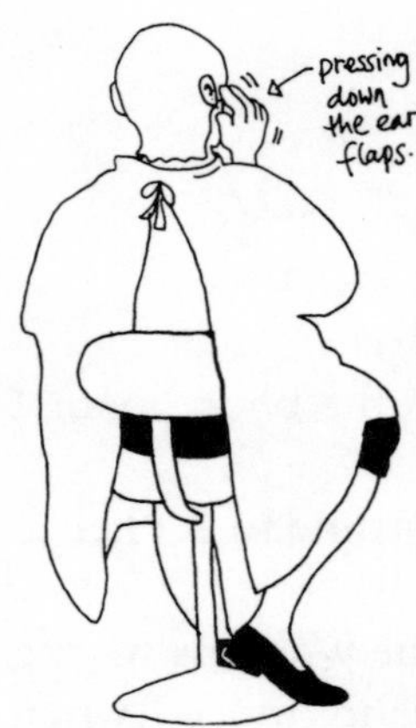

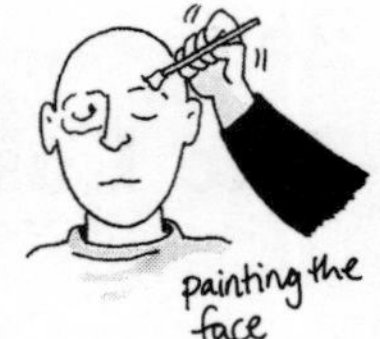

totally smooth although, as everybody chatted throughout the whole operation, the paste was obviously fairly elastic. The whole operation lasted about ten minutes. The cap, (needless to say) snipped, glued and covered with gunk, is not re-usable.

Bob Smith chatted to me while he was being done: 'Some of the lads had their hair cut short for this,' he said (not him, mind you) 'and no facial hair, of course. The white stuff is water-based. I mean it comes off.' He added reassuringly, 'I painted somebody's entire body with it last week.'

Mike left his chair looking particularly gleaming and studied the effect in the mirror. 'Yup, I think this is Cap of the Week,' he said eventually. 'We have very strict criteria, you know. Adhevisness, look, comfort.'

'And triple toe loop,' said Bob, who'd obviously been watching the skating on TV.

Up on stage Brian was looking for weights, the statues in *Rosenkavalier* had run through all the round-shaped ones and he'd been jamming the ordinary square ones into their bases. Now it appeared that these weights, and the statues, had totally disappeared and there was nothing left to steady the back wall except Laurie. Another tech was dispatched to hunt up strays. He found a fine crop doing duty as door stops in the dressing rooms near the stage.

Louise passed me on her way to open the show while Chris disappeared, as usual, into the farthest reaches of the OP to sing '*Under thy shade*'. Presumably he does this to loosen up. I went over to the PS and noticed, sadly, that the packing boxes were already out, just behind the Prop Tray. Bob joined me. 'Oh dear,' he said, 'It's the last one. I really love this show.' The other Wardens were looking rather glum as well.

Amanda began to dish out canes to the Beginners. 'Hurry along, please,' she said to a bunch of Chorus who were chatting US. One bloke flapped his hand graciously: 'Don't hold the show for me,' he said. But Bob was less relaxed; he'd got caught behind some woolgatherers. 'Let me on!' he cried.

Act I ran faultlessly, from the technical point of view, though it was quite evident the cast were having a high old time. Mark Richardson did his Ian Richardson impression at the Investiture and Nerys and Yvonne made such a meal of '*If you'd seduce him*' that the faces on the TV monitor looked positively animated. By Act II even the Wardens had cheered up; Mike had made a card for one of the girls which he stuck in her cake and the Chorus did their best to corpse the waiters with such witticisms as, 'No, we won't have any coffee after all' 'Do you take credit cards?' and other hallowed gags. Amanda discovered later that their cups, usually empty in this show, had actually contained something to drink – not, it would seem, coffee . . .

The Bridge, ever sensitive to the prevailing mood, collapsed with a dreadful clang; everybody in the PS winced. 'We're going out with a bang,' said Mark Holmes. He added that my presence was required in the Wardens' dressing room. I followed him down at the end of the Act and discovered that Mike had drawn a caricature of me, dash it, which (briefly) made me see things from the victim's point of view.

The PS was buzzing with good cheer at the start of Act III although I was saddened to see Brian packing away props, as they became redundant, into the bases of the Parterre. The scene looked rather like the end of Andy Pandy. The coffee lamps were already off the tables and stacked on the LX stairs. 'It'll take eight guys to lift this when it's full,' said Brian grimly as he rammed in some of the red ropes.

Terry Lyddall (the PS magic door man) and Amanda took my mind of this depressing sight by leafing through the sketch pad. 'That looks like Nick,' said Terry of the drawing Carl took such exception to. 'He's got great plates of meat.'

Terry striking the cake.

I drew a picture of Terry, eating some of the cake, and knocked off thumbnails of all the people who had escaped me so far. Chris was waiting to go on and got himself added to the list.

'Don't worry, you have *carte blanche*,' he said amiably as he saw me scrunch up a cartoon as too unfair (I wondered if this would stand up in a court of law) and disappeared on to the stage, to sing '*Ah, love, tyrannic love*,' in what must have been an improvisatory frame of mind.

'Oh dear, he's still in his Munich mood,' murmured Amanda, as an animal howl ended the aria, however a huge round of applause followed him off, and he remarked as he left that he could have done with a few more shows.

The Generals cheated outrageously in the bowls match; Mark Richardson kicked the jack away from the other guys' bowls, and immediately found Roger Begley kicking it away even further to make sure *he* didn't win either. Meanwhile Jean had decided to change the policy of a lifetime and alter the *sotto voce* message she gives Arsamenes just before the Quarrel Duet.[1] On she went to whisper in his ear and Chris's immediate double-take (and hastily swallowed grin) made us all curious to know what on earth she could have said.

Louise smashed the busts for the last time – they sounded like mini explosions tonight – and we were into the curtain calls all too soon. The audience gave the opera an immense send-off, starting off with a mighty 'Bravo!' for the Wardens and the Chorus and cheering and stamping their approval as each principal came out for their solo bows (see photo 'Final Call'). Then, suddenly, the Tab was down and the wing full of chorus, actors and principals, embracing everybody in sight, and marching off down to their dressing rooms in a flurry of hugs and farewells.

Jane summed it up in her last Stage report – 'An absolutely fabulous show!'

Note

1 This is actually written out for her in the Prompt Book: 'I have a warning for you from Romilda – Xerxes wants you killed.'

Appendix I
Opera seria

Handel's *Xerxes* (*Serse*, in Italian) was first performed at the King's Theatre, Haymarket in 1738. It was based on an earlier Venetian opera of the same name, performed in 1645 and composed by Cavalli. Handel clearly liked the style of the original and kept many of its Venetian features: a fast moving plot, short arias, and a predominantly comic tone, however, as he tidied the piece up into an *opera seria* it is as such that we should first approach it.

Opera seria (serious opera) is the term applied to any opera written in the early part of the eighteenth century which has an Italian libretto, a formal musical structure, and an overwhelming interest in the solo voice.

There was a huge interest in virtuoso singing at the time, which *opera seria* was expressly designed to accomodate, and the modern ear, in listening to one, is immediately struck by the almost total absence of concerted singing. The only ensembles you could expect were a couple of duets for the lovers, and a final *coro*, (a simple chorus set to a dance rhythm) sung by the principals at the close of the show and, though an actual chorus was sometimes employed in Handel's later operas, their contribution was effectively limited to a few short numbers in praise of the hero. The greater part of the evening was devoted to solo arias.

The arias followed a set format, indeed, their very place in the plot was a matter of tight theatrical etiquette. In 1726, Giuseppe Riva (an Italian living in England) jotted down the formula that a prospective librettist for the King's Theatre, Haymarket needed to follow, given the star singers available:

> 'For this year there must be two equal parts in the operas for Cuzzoni and Faustina; Senesino is the chief male character, and his part must be heroic; the other three male parts must proceed by degrees with three arias each, one in each Act.

The duet should be at the end of the second Act, and between the two ladies.'

Actually this particular formula (based apparently on Handel's *Ottone*) would have been a disaster, as 'the two ladies' – Cuzzoni and Faustina – came to blows on the Haymarket stage a year later but Riva's approach to the construction of an opera was typical: all European theatres ran a star system and were equally careful to distribute arias according to the hierarchical position of their singers.

This involved a great deal more than just handing out the lion's share of the arias to the *prima donna* and the *primo uomo* (the female and male lead singers). The star performers would expect arias that showed off their technical ability and any composer who was deemed to have let them down in this respect could expect the outraged singer to produce an *aria di baule* (literally, a suitcase aria, one that was carried around with them) that did do them justice, and which could be inserted in the opera at a suitably prominent moment.

Handel rarely gave in to this sort of behaviour but then he was particularly good at tailoring his music to suit individual performers and, though he once threatened to throw a particularly temperamental diva out of the window, he was on the whole easy-going about singers' personal whims. He upgraded the social status of a character in *Radamisto*, for example, when the singer was heard to complain 'That he had never acted . . . in any other Opera below the Character of a Sovereign', and he re-wrote an aria in *Ottone* which Anastasia Robinson, Handel's English prima donna, considered too fiery for her plaintive talents.

It was, in any case, prudent to indulge your singers. Handel employed first class talent – indeed Senesino, his lead *castrato* was one of the most sought-after singers of his day. A *castrato* is just what it sounds like, a man who had been castrated. This was an Italian custom, originating in the general ban on women singers in church and, in Rome, on the stage. It was usually performed on musically gifted boys before puberty and their unbroken voices, thus artificially preserved, often developed into instruments of exceptional brilliance and power. First-rate *castrati* were international favourites and commanded high fees, while their prominence in the ranks of *opera seria* gave the genre an exotic glamour – and its overwhelming interest in the high voice.

Most of the characters in *opera seria*, male and female, were sopranos or altos; this included all the lovers (by far the largest category in the cast list) and such villains as could combine villainy with love-making.

The lower voices attracted much less attention. Tenors made brief appearances in early Handel as villainous fathers but it was only when a couple of gifted tenors (Annibale Fabri and John Beard) came Handel's way that he created any major roles for them. The sympathetic emperors in *Poro* and *Tamerlano* were writen for tenors (one was even entrusted with the second love interest in *Ariodante*) but even so, it is not a prominent voice in *opera seria*, whereas most operas contain at least one bass. Handel used basses to provide a touch of vocal contrast and to play the (elderly) sovereigns, the generals or the more abandoned villains – they were needed, anyway, to sing the bottom line in the final *coro*. In spite of their rather unimportant position, it comes as something of a surprise to find, in *Amadigi di Gaula*, that in 1715 Handel apparently did not have one at all; he gave the part of the heroine's uncle (who wraps up the plot) to a soprano. Oddly enough, a bass was cast as the eponymous hero in one of Handel's last operas, *Imeneo*, where he actually walks off with the girl; one is tempted to date the decline of *opera seria* from this moment.

This aberration aside, the overriding interest in *opera seria* is set firmly in the stratosphere, in the soprano and mezzo-soprano and contralto voices of the women, or the soprano and alto of the *castrati*. In *Xerxes* the romantic male leads are Arsamenes, an alto, and Xerxes himself, a very high alto, practically a soprano. Indeed, as originally cast, Xerxes was played by a *castrato* and Arsamenes by a woman, which highlights another oddity of *opera seria* – the high incidence of travesty roles. Travesty literally means 'disguise' and a travesty part is one in which a woman is either disguised as a man (like Rosalind/Ganymede in *As You Like It*) or actually plays one. The latter is more usual in *opera seria* where a woman might find herself playing such unambiguously male roles as Julius Ceasar, Alexander the Great or Richard I.

Handel wrote some 26 male parts specificaly for women and, though he preferred to cast a first-class *castrato* as the hero, in the absence of a Senesino he invariably cast a woman. Second-rate *castrati* were no sort of draw. In the first cast of *Radamisto*, for example, the two principal male leads were played by women (the castrato only getting the third part) and similarly, in the original *Xerxes*, though Xerxes himself was played by a *castrato*, (Caffarelli) the part of the principal lover was given to Maria Marchesini, a specialist in travesty. Pitch was everything in *opera seria*, lovers had to have high voices and the 'natural' high male voice, the tenor, was apparently no substitute.

The taste for the high voice may in fact have preceded the fashion for *castrati*; the sixteenth century, at least, seems to share it. Shakespeare, for example, is clearly thinking of a flawed bell when Hamlet asks the Player Queen (an adolescent boy in the original play) if his voice is yet 'cracked within the ring', while Arviragus, in *Cymbeline*, laments that his voice has 'the mannish crack' when he excuses his singing of the dirge for Imogen. Be that as it may, the travesty tradition was well established in Handel's day and the women who specalised in male parts were very popular. Doubtless cross-dressing, then, as now, had its own peculiar fascination.

However, whether the singer was a *castrato* or a woman soprano, passionate or melancholy, covered in chains or carried in triumph, the aria he or she sung was invariably of one basic type, the *da capo*.

Da capo means, literally, 'from the top' and refers to the fact that at some point in the aria the singer will be instructed to go back to the top of the page and repeat the first section. But a *da capo* aria entails more than the mere repetition of a tune; its text, music, even its place in the action, were controlled by a set of conventions.

An aria was supposed to move between one specific emotion and its complementary mood and, coming at the climax of the preceding scene, gave a chance for the character particularly involved to tell the audience how he or she was feeling. In Handel operas they are used as building blocks to describe the inner life of the characters. However, as not all librettists could come up with an appropriate emotion to close every scene, Handel – and many other lesser talents – were often obliged to fall back on a metaphor aria.

The metaphor aria was still a *da capo* but the text was unspecific about the passion involved. Instead it compared the singer's feelings to something else: a ship tossed in a storm, perhaps, or a stream finding its way to the sea. Handel used them when the plot was not throwing up a strong enough situation, and a great deal of incidental natural knowledge can be gleaned from their texts. Guido in *Flavio*, for example, compares himself to the noble ermine – an animal notorious for the distress it feels if its fur gets muddied – or Ruggerio, in *Alcina*, feels the complex emotions of a Hyrcanian tigress – torn between flying from her foes, or staying to defend her cubs.

The great advantage of this type of *da capo* was that it could be inserted into more or less any opera; most 'suitcase arias' were of the metaphor variety. They were also particularly prone to having an expressive *obbligato* accompaniment; that is, a solo instrument, standing out from the orchestra and accompanying the voice by winding in and out of the vocal line. The aria from *Giuilo Cesare* in which Caesar compares Cleopatra's voice to a lark has a solo violin *obbligato*, soaring above the voice and suggesting a lark singing as it flies.

However, whatever the subject of the aria, the text had to follow a specific pattern: an emotion, a reflection on it, and then the main emotion again and, in doing so, perfectly followed the structure of the music.

A *da capo* was introduced by an orchestral passage, the *ritornello*, which was followed by the first part of the aria, the 'A' section; this described the particular emotion that impelled the character to sing in the first place, and was in turn followed by a shorter passage in a contrasted key, the 'B' section. This was usually a comment on the main emotion, or set up an emotion complementary to it. Then, *da capo* – back to the top, the 'A' section was sung again. However, this time, the tune was not merely repeated but embellished, the singer adding whatever runs and cadenzas he thought suitable to heighten the emotion (and display his virtuosity) then, waiting only for another *ritornello* to round off the piece, he exited to thunderous applause.

The Exit after the aria was inviolable; in fact *da capos* were often referred to as Exit Arias, and, though it might seem disconcerting in theory to have a major character leave the stage every ten minutes, it does not necessarily come across like that in the theatre. A well-constructed *opera seria* scene will culminate in its aria, and the exit will therefore appear inevitable. Of course it is difficult to write a plot which consists of a succession of scenes each of which ends in an emotional climax and an exit, but the eighteenth century librettists showed considerable ingenuity, not to say cunning, in contriving their action to fit this pattern. The only times one notices the artificiality of the convention is when the librettist fails to provide a convincing exit for a villain who, after plainly expressing his intention to murder or rape one of the good characters, clears off – leaving his victims unharmed.

In fact all *opera seria* was made up of threatened action, rather than actual deeds of violence. This is partly because the emotions

provoked by potential danger are more interesting than mere slaughter, and partly because, with only half a dozen principals at his disposal, no composer could really afford to kill his characters off. In F*lavio* and *Amadigi di Gaula*, where the fights take an uncharacteristically fatal turn, Handel is obliged to have the 'dead' singer fill out his part in the final *coro* from the wings; it is worth noting that the corpse in both these operas is those of the villain, or the non essential bass. The hero and the heroine bear charmed lives to ensure that the opera has the proper Happy Ending.

This convention is traditionally ascribed to Frederick the Great (who apparently objected that tragic endings put him off his supper) but in fact the mood of the age was against tragedy. Lacking any robust belief in the interaction of the natural and supernatural worlds, the eighteenth century liked to see Virtue triumphant here on earth, Princes magnaminous and lovers happy. Even Dr Johnson approved of Garrick's acting edition of *King Lear*, in which Cordelia is saved.

Xerxes, as one of Handel's late operas – and a comedy – takes its *opera seria* format quite lightly; even so, its scenes are all constructed according to these conventions, and it will be worth while running through the few remaining technical terms used to describe them.

A scene in *opera seria* is usually made up of a passage of *secco* (dry or spare) recitative leading up to a *da capo* aria. Winton Dean's description of Handelian recitative as 'the maximum of action in the minimum of music,' cannot be bettered; it is of course the part of the opera that advances the plot. During the recitative the characters talk to each other, make love, threaten their foes and (until well into the final Act) get hold of the wrong end of the stick. The music during these passages is set to ordinary speech rhythms and its simple vocal line is accompanied by a harpsichord with a handful of other instruments. (In the ENO *Xerxes* the recitative was accompanied by the harpsichord, and a cello with a double bass or a bassoon adding extra colour in some passages.) These minute forces are called the *continuo* group, and the abbreviated music they play as they accompany the singers is described as *secco* – dry, spare. When the action becomes especially tense the composer may accompany the recitative with the orchestra (usually comprising the *continuo* and the strings); this is called 'accompanied recitative' and its appearance invariably raises the emotional temperature of the piece.

This completes the formal structure of *opera seria*, and the reader will perhaps have gathered that one of the great strengths of the genre was its very formality. It proved extraordinarily easy in the opera house to defeat expectation by the minutest deviation from the rules, and an adept composer could produce a powerful dramatic effect by doing so.

Xerxes is sometimes described as Handel's only comic opera[1] – it certainly contains his only servant in the *buffo* (comic) tradition. However, many of his other noble characters are treated with the same gentle irony as the cast of *Xerxes*, and Handel is as adroit as W S Gilbert in the comic denouement. Partenope, Aggripina, Ezio, Flavio, even the heroic Giulio Cesare, rely either on a sudden turn of fortune – or an equally sudden wave of remorse – to save the day. What is unusual in *Xerxes* is the consistent comic mood, and the relaxed way in which Handel treats the *opera seria* conventions; at least half the arias are not in *da capo* form at all; a couple of indignant singers bounce into their arias without waiting for the *ritornello*, and the lovers use their one duet to have so blazing a row that it spills over into their next patch of recitative.

Some odd moments in the plot, as when Arsamenes exits after one aria, only to walk straight back on again (he is needed in the next scene) can be put down to the normal difficulties of writing within the *opera seria* convention however, when the *da capo* in a couple of arias is repeated not once but three times, it is difficult not to believe that Handel himself is teasing the audience, and that *opera seria* itself is being sent up. Indeed Xerxes' final *bravura* aria sounds at once formidable and a parody of every operatic invocation you have ever heard to the Furies.

Handel's mood, sympathetic and mocking, was perfectly caught by Nicholas Hytner's production for ENO. He decided to respect the *opera seria* conventions, while presenting the opera as a comedy and the result was a classic comedy of manners in which Handel's gentle irony was matched by Hytner's quiet allusions to contemporary England.

Note

1 Though a case could be made for the prevailing comic mood in *Agrippina*, *Amadigi*, *Flavio* and *Partenope*.

Appendix II
The Historical Xerxes

Xerxes is the biblical Ahasuerus, he is mentioned in *Ezra* 4:6 and figures as the rather improbable king in the book of *Esther*.

He ruled Persia 486–465 BC and appears to have been a man of considerably less ability than his famous father, Darius. After bridging the Hellespont, and capturing Athens, most of his European ventures went wrong and his Aegean fleet was destroyed. He was eventually assassinated and succeeded by a younger son, Artaxerxes.

Xerxes (and Darius) have left the Hall of Audience at Persepolis to posterity and, though it was destroyed by Alexander the Great in 331 BC, its 13 columns (of an original 72) are still an impressive sight; photographs of the site now look uncannily like the *Xerxes* set.

Herodotus records that during Xerxes' campaign in Greece he marched across the Phrygian/Lydian border and, 'he came across a plane tree of such beauty that he was moved to decorate it with golden ornaments and to leave behind one of his Immortals to guard it.'

Xerxes 'then prepared to move forward to Abydos, where a bridge had already been constructed across the Hellespont from Asia to Europe . . . but a subsequent storm of great violence smashed it up and carried everything away.' Xerxes was furious and ordered the Hellespont to be given 300 lashes ('typical of a barbarous nation', comments Herodotus) while his engineers constructed another bridge over which his army marched successfully, in spite of an ominous eclipse.

Xerxes *was* married to an 'Amestris' and we hear that one of his brothers, Arsamenes, commanded the Utian and Myci regiments under him. After his Greek campaign he entertained a disastrous passion for the wife of another of his brothers.

Herodotus records a moment when Xerxes showed he was

something more than The Persian Tyrant. On his march on Greece he paused at Abydos to hold a review and

> looking down over the shore was able to see the whole of his army and navy at a single view. Suddenly as he watched them he was seized with a whim to witness a rowing match. The match took place and was won by the Phoenicians of Sidon, to the great delight of Xerxes who was as pleased with the race as with his army. Still the king watched the spectacle below, and when he saw the whole Hellespont hidden by ships, and all the beaches of Abydos and all the open ground filled with men, he congratulated himself – and the moment after burst into tears. His uncle Artabanus asked him why he wept. 'I was thinking,' Xerxes replied, 'and it came into my mind how pitifully short human life is, for of all these thousands of men not one will be alive in a hundred years' time.'

There is an echo of this incident in Byron's famous description of Xerxes seated on the base of Mount Aegaleos watching his fleet's defeat at Salamis:

> A king sate on the rocky brow
> Which looks o'er sea-born Salamis;
> And ships, by thousands, lay below,
> And men in nations; – all were his!
> He counted them at break of day -
> And when the sun set where were they?
>
> (*Don Juan*, Canto III, stanza 86)

Many of the cast appeared to have looked up their historical counterparts. Jean Rigby chilled my blood during an LBH rehearsal by telling me all the ghastly things the historical Amastris had done to the unfortunate souls who got in her way. Ann Murray (the original Xerxes in this production) said of the Finale; 'I thought, there he is, head of all those armies. One and a half million, wasn't it? And he can't get the girl . . .'

Illustrations

1 ENO Prompt Copy
The 'O' marks in the score refer to the moves noted on the opposite page.

AS XERXES SITS – ALL SIT
WAITER X'S US WITH
TROLLEY

WAITER

XERXES

X

ATALANTA

O POINTS AT CAKE
ON TROLLEY OP OF HIM
WAITER SERVES + STEPS
BACK

O AT. STANDS COUPLE OF
PACES TO XER. TABLE

O GIVES XER. LETTER

O AT. X's BACK TO OP
OF DSPS TABLE

2 ENO Prompt Copy
Atalanta's moves in the Coffee House Scene.
'X' means cross. 'Waiter X's US' means Waiter crosses up stage.

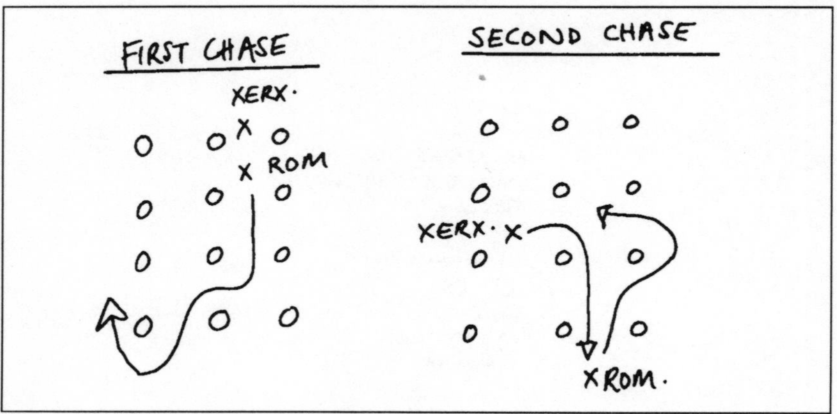

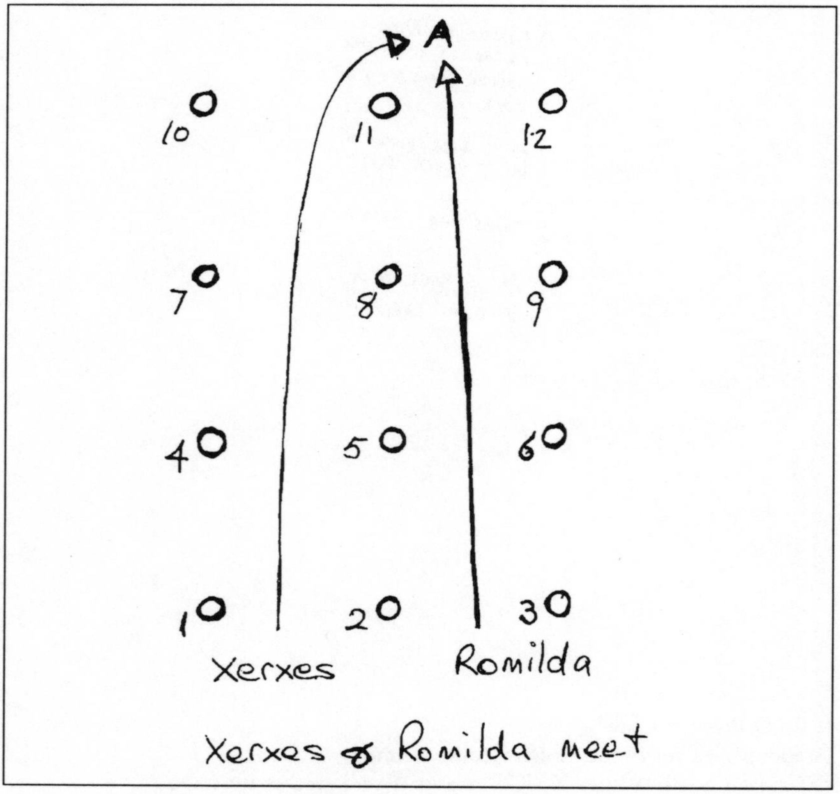

A
10 11 12
7 8 9
4 5 6
1 2 3
Xerxes Romilda

Xerxes & Romilda meet

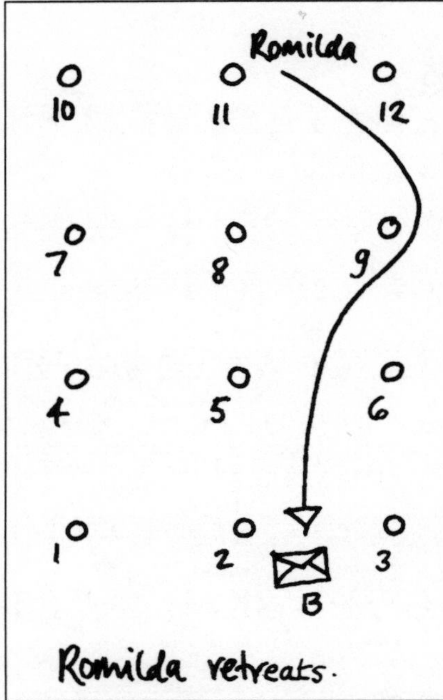

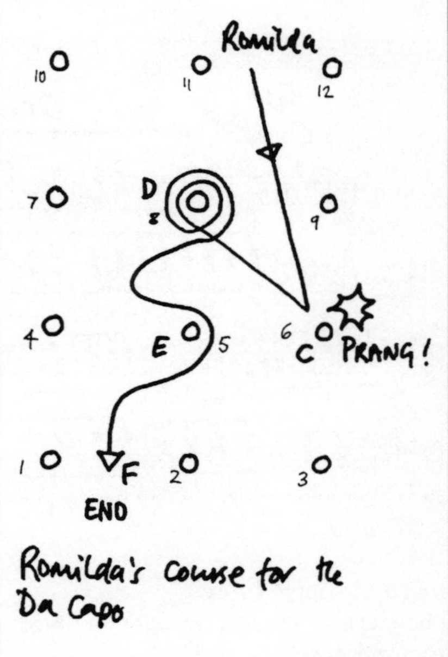

3 Diagrams for the Cactus Run.

*14 No. 27 may be transposed down a tone into G major for a Countertenor.

4 ENO Prompt Copy
The start of '*If you'd worship* . . . ' Notice the cue line that runs across from the opposite page.

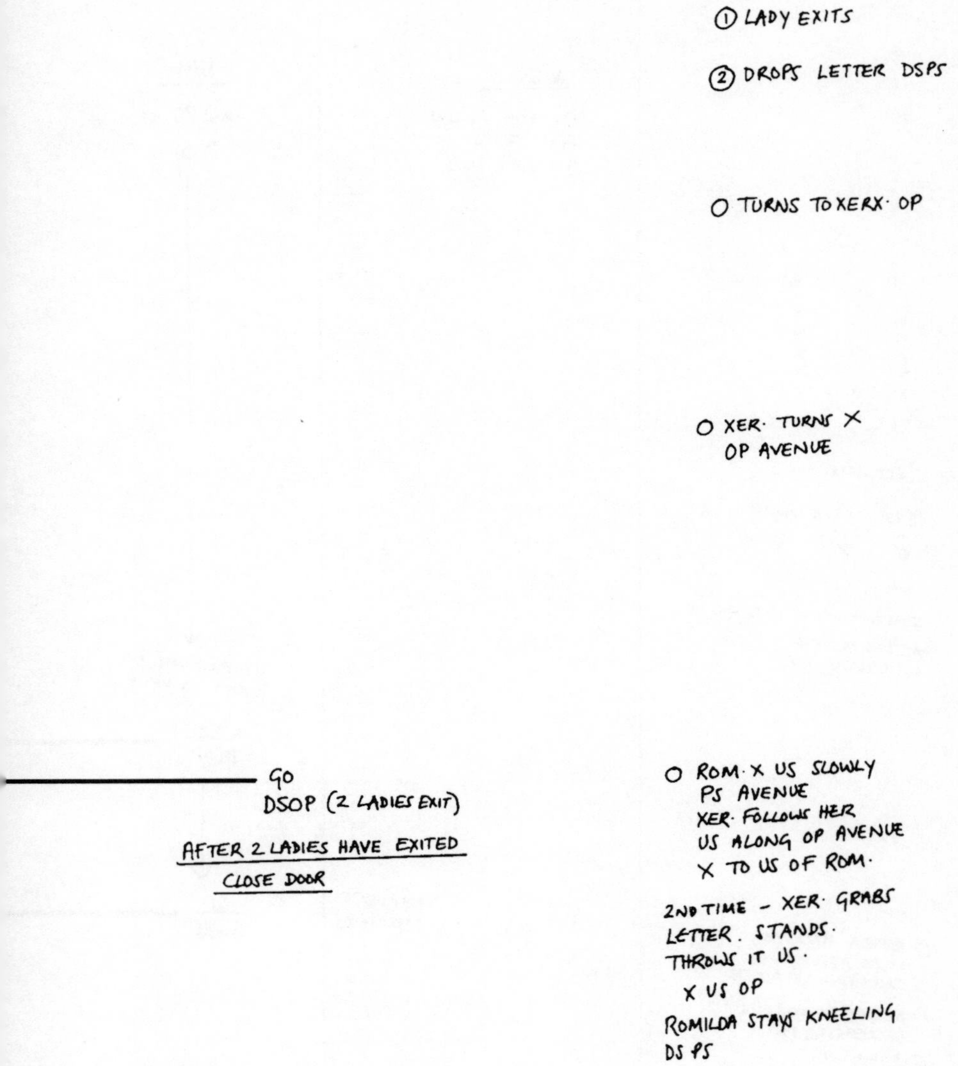

① LADY EXITS

② DROPS LETTER DSPS

O TURNS TO XERX· OP

O XER· TURNS X
OP AVENUE

GO
DSOP (2 LADIES EXIT)

AFTER 2 LADIES HAVE EXITED
CLOSE DOOR

O ROM· X US SLOWLY
PS AVENUE
XER· FOLLOWS HER
US ALONG OP AVENUE
X TO US OF ROM·

2ND TIME – XER· GRABS
LETTER. STANDS·
THROWS IT US·
X US OP
ROMILDA STAYS KNEELING
DS PS

5 ENO Prompt Copy
The line running across from the score indicates a cue for the beginning of the aria. In this case it is a 'Go' for the DS OP door.

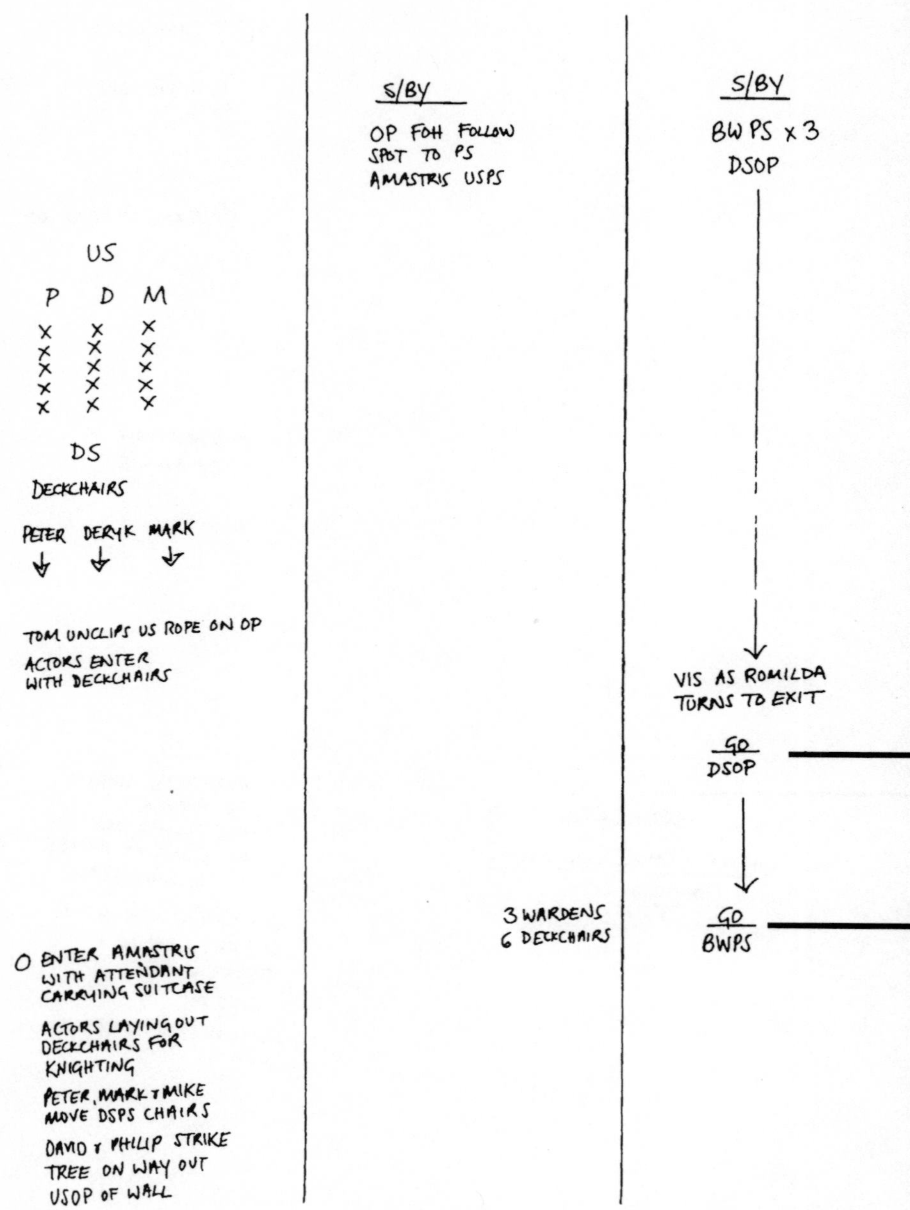

6 The beginning of the Investiture Scene. The X's on the left indicate deck chairs. Note the 'Standby' line meeting its 'Go' line in the column nearest the score.

7 ENO Prompt Copy.
Note that the lines end in two vertical lines on a note. The cue happens on this note – though the second one is marked 'vis' (visual). The DSM will in this case give the 'Go' when she *sees* Romilda turn.

8 ENO Prompt Copy.
The beginning of the Storm Scene. The side TVs are turned off so that the light from the screens does not glow on the darkened stage.

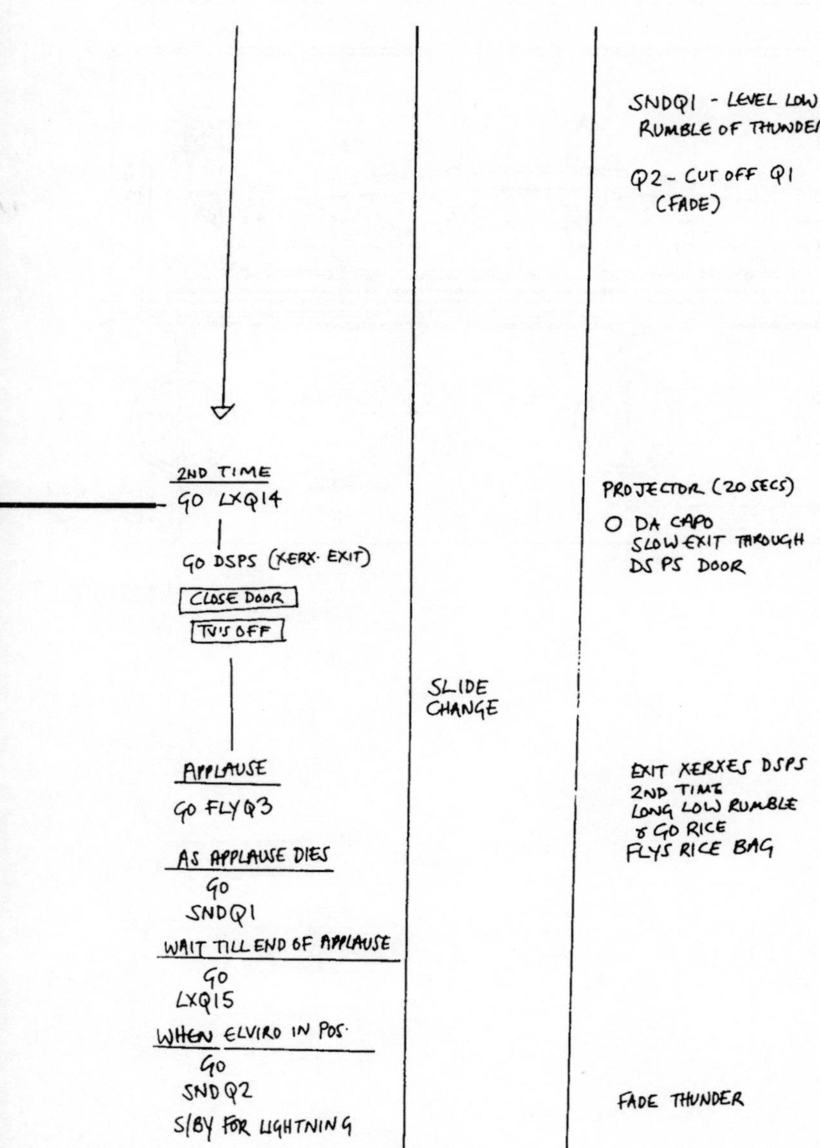

9 ENO Prompt Copy.
Cues for the Storm Scene. 'Q' means cue, 'LX' means Electrics (Lighting), SND means Sound. What these cues represent (thunder, rice, etc.) is described in the far right column.

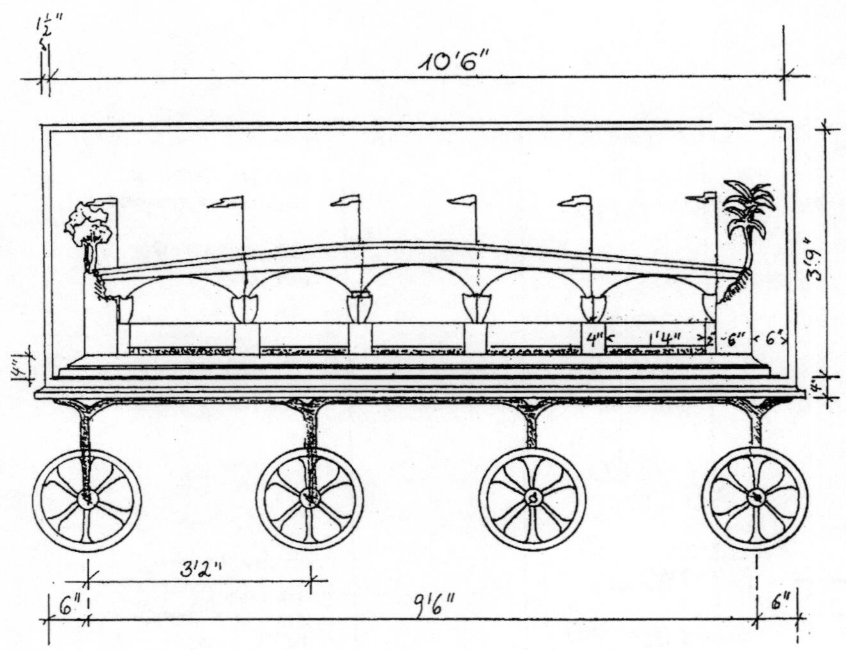

9b The blue print of Xerxes' bridge. Notice the little trees at each end.

My beloved,

Ah, how my heart aches as I live out this cruel exile

No moment passes without tearful memories of thy fair face causing me to cry out thy name

My treacherous brother shall not prevail, oh my dearest

Remain true to me as I remain thy devoted Arsamenes.

10 Arsamenes' letter to Romilda. This prop is never actually read out so the Prop Department can use their imaginations.

<u>WEDNESDAY 29TH DECEMBER</u>

XERXES
10.30 Winter Kenny
11.00 + Rigby
12.00 + Robson
12.30 + Jones Napier-Burrows Richardson
LBH 1 IB ND EJ BH

- - - - - - - - - - - - - - - - - - - -

2.30 FULL CAST **<u>RUN</u>**
ACTORS
LBH 1 IB ND EJ BH

<u>ROSENKAVALIER</u>
10.30 EvansBurgess Ball Dyer Newman Kestner
Walker
[Choristers leave 1.00]
LBH 3 JMYK ML DR LH NK

11.00 Naoumenko **<u>2WIDS</u>**
LBHB YK ML HRB NK

<u>ROSENKAVALIER MUSIC</u>
2.30 FULL CAST TO BE DETAILED
LBH3 YK ML HRB NK

<u>5.30</u> **<u>LOHENGRIN</u>**
ME TL SH CM GH MHp
RJs (ML)

11 Call Sheet for the 29 December. The times the singers are called is shown on the left against their surnames. The venue (LBH Studio 1) is shown below with the initials of the music and production staff involved.

Act One Scene One

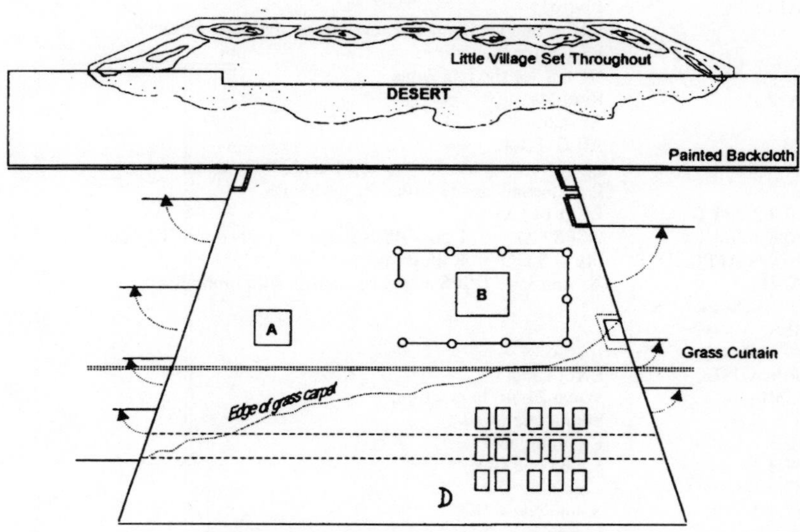

Opposite Prompt	ONSTAGE	Prompt Side
Glass of port on round silver tray (Warden) Small silver spade with soil (Holmes) Black cane with silver top and Xerxes gloves (Warden) 8 Grey walking canes (Chorus	A) **Large tree in tub.** B) **Statue of Handel.** C) **10 whitepost, 9 red ropes.** D) **15 folded deckchairs,** ***set so that chair faces upstage when opened.*** **Red Marks-Poles & Tree** **Black Marks-Deckchairs**	White Xerxes chair with pile of 40 concert programmes. 2 White poles for tree. 8 Grey Walking canes.

12 Prop plan for the Concert Scene.

STAGE MANAGERS RUNNING PLOT CONTINUED P.8

CALL:	Elviro	
	Ladies and Gentlemen actors for the umbrella entrance	
	PS LX for the lighting	
	OP LX for the rain spots	
CALL:	Romilda	
	Amastris	
	All G Actors	
	Stage Techniciana for the USPS and DSOP doors	
	Prop technicians to strike the bridge PS.	
170.3.3 2nd T	LXQ 14 GO	
170.3.4 2nd T	DSPS GO	Door OPENS, Xerxes exits door CLOSES
170 ON APPLAUSE	Fly Q 3 GO	Rain starts
170VIS	As rain sarts USPS actors run across with umbrellas	
170 AS APPLAUSE DIES		
170 END OF APPLAUSE	LXQ 15 GO	
171VIS	When Elviro in position;	
	Sound cue GO	
177.3.1	Lightning GO	
177.3.2	Sound cue GO	
177.4.1	Lightning GO	
177.4.3	Sound cue 4 GO	
	Lightning GO	
177.5.2	Sound cue 5 GO	
	Lightning GO	
	BRIDGE BREAKS	
CALL;	Arsemenes	
	Elviro	
	Warden for the hedge cutting	
	OP LX for the tree plugging up.	
	All stage and prop technicians for the doors and striking of the deckchairs	
	Wardrobe to collect the knighting sword and Xerxes gloves from the OP.	
67.3.1.2nd T	LXQ 6 GO	
	CSPS GO	Hedge door OPEN
	CSOP GO	Hedge door OPEN
76.3.42nd T	Fly Q 3 GO	Hedge in to the deck
67VIS	When cloth hits the deck	
	MSOP GO	Door OPENS and STAYS OPEN
	USOP GO	Winged God exits fast door STAYS OPEN
	USPS GO	Door OPENS, Ladder with Hedge warden up it entrance, Door stays OPEN
67VIS	When Ladder set;	
	Fly Q 4 GO	Hedge in to Hedge dead fast
67VIS	When Hedge to Hedge dead;	
	LXQ 6.2 GO	
67VIS	As applause dies;	
	DSOP GO	Door OPENS, Arsemenes and Elviro entrance, Elviro exits Door CLOSE

13 Stage Manager's running plot for the Storm Scene. The numbers on the left refer to the relevant page number in the score and the cue number. The Stage Manager is not *giving* these cues, she is making sure they happen.

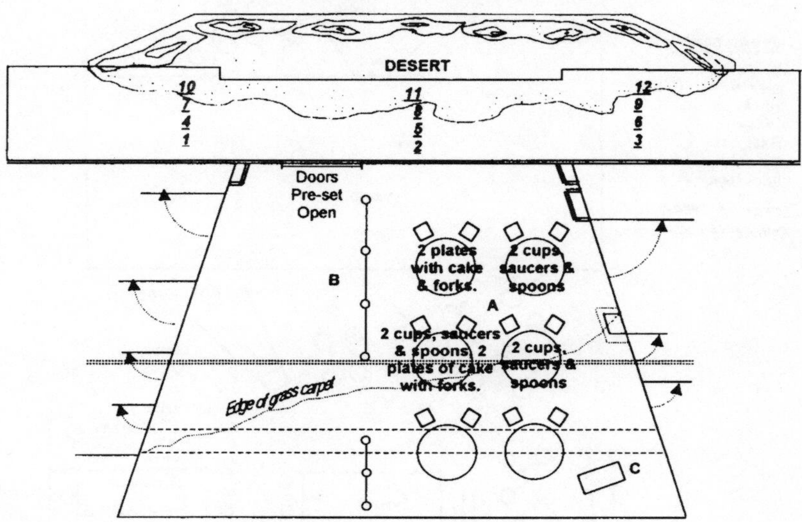

Opposite Prompt	ONSTAGE	Prompt Side
Canvas bag with pink & white carnations & letter "My Beloved". 6 Walking Canes (Chorus)	A) **6 round tables with 2 silver chairs at each. Fixed lamp on each table. Plates etc, set as above.** B) **7 white posts, 5 red ropes.** C) **Dessert trolley with 2 prop cakes, 1 real sliced cake, 5 plates with 1 slice of cake & 1 fork on each (2 different sorts of cake) 1 pile of plates and forks.** ***Upstage of Backcloth for Scene 2: 12 Cacti in pots.***	Tray with full decanter (apple juice) & 2 glasses. Tray with 1 cup, saucer & teaspoon. Tray with 2 cups, saucers, & teaspoons. 6 cups, saucers, teaspoons. Empty tray.

14 Prop plan for the Coffee House Scene.

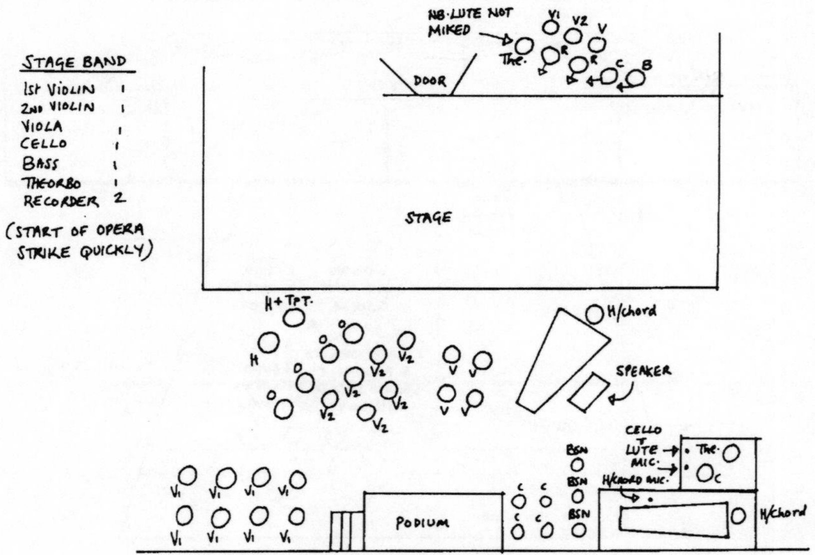

15 Sound plan for the Orchestra and off-stage Orchestra. The instruments of the orchestra are reduced to letters and numbers (V1 is Violin 1) and the speakers and microphones are indicated.

Page number in the score

SHOW:XERXES ENOSOUND Q SHEET DATE:JAN 94

P	Q	ACTION
		ACT 2
111		LUTE MIC Odb → level = 0 decibels
112		OFF
121		LUTE MIC -5db → level = −5 decibels
128		OFF
144		LUTE MIC Odb
150		OFF
ON	ST/BY	DC @ 0 DC 3 @-15 ← switching on the faders
170	Q1	HIT KG3 CRASH AND RUMBLE KG4 DELAYED RUMBLE
	Q2	FADE OFF DC 3
WHEN	FINISHED	RESET DC 3 @ - 15, ADD M5+6 TO CH'S 12&13 (L&R)
177	Q3 Q4 FADE	HIT KG5 RUMBLE OFF DC3
WHEN	FINISHED	RESET DC 3 @ ODB
	Q5	HIT KG1 CRASH KG2 EXPL
	RESET	DESELECT M 5+6 AND 9+10 ON CH'S 12 & 13 (OPS 3+4)
ON ST/BY		DC 2 OFF, DC 3 @ - 10
180	Q6 F/O	HIT KG5 RUMBLE FADE OFF - OFF BY THE TIME PILLARS ARE WAY IN

KG= Key group: 2 sounds happen together, so 2 keys are involved.

16 Sound sheet for the whole opera.

English National Opera

Opera Xerxes **Performance No** 47 (last in series)
Theatre Coliseum **Date** Thursday, 24th February 1994

Act	Scene	Orchestra Rung in	Orchestra Ready	FOH Ready	National Anthem	Curtain Up	Curtain Down	Playing Time	Scene Change	Interval
1		6.35	6.59	7.01	7.03	7.08	8.12	1hr 4		
										21 m
2		8.25	8.31			8.33	9.37	1hr 4		
										15 m
3		9.43	9.51			9.52	10.35	43		

Total time 3 Hrs 36 Mins Houselights: 10.39

DUTY H.O.D's	Stage	Mr. Parker	LX	Mr. Currier		Props	

Absentees, Cast or Chorus Changes, etc (with reasons)

Remarks

When the bridge was un-veiled the front bar came down as well.

A fabulous show.

2 Full Calls

Signed Jane Randall Seen by [signature]
Stage Manager

17 Show report for 24 February. All the timings from the first orchestra bell are recorded plus any technical hitches. This was clearly a very good performance.

TO: Peter Jones, David Pountney, Jeremy Caulton, Jane Randall, Mandy Burnett, Angie Smith, Laurence Holderness, Ted Murphy, Ray Sheppard, Ivy Cannell, Gill Dixon, Dewi Evans, Pam Orange, Karen Crichton, Mark Dakin, Spencer Parker, Andrew Joslin

SHOW WATCH REPORT

XERXES – Thursday, 20 February 1992

Seat: O/S R12

A packed house saw a brilliant show, full of fine music and exciting singing. I fell in love with this show in Kiev on the first night of the Tour to the erstwhile Soviet Union and it hasn't lost its magic

ACT III

1) As we know, the set is now in need of considerable refurbishment as many of the pieces no longer fit together smoothly, particularly on the OP. This show deserves a face-lift to restore it to its original perfection of line.

2) There was a crash backstage just before "I shall declare my passion".

3) There was a large chip out of the Parterre, in the middle, between the bottom two drawers.

ACT II

4) Great applause for the setting of the cacti for Scene 2. The tallest cactus on the US end of the middle line is very wobbly and is keeling over, but it did get a laugh.

5) The rice/rain comes in gusts rather than a steady pour but the Storm Scene with its evocative lighting is a wonderful effect.

ACT III

6) The noise and wobbling of the egg as it crosses the stage is a pity as it contrasts with the elegant and precise smoothness of all the other in-view changes carried-out by the Flunkies. I find the untidiness of the hedge a little irritating for similar reasons (the unevenness of the gathers at the bottom and the fact that it catches every time it flies in and out).

7) The OP doors were sometimes slammed rather than smoothly shut.

8) The Griffin light was taken out after snapping on and off several times.

9) The shadow of a rope swung-out across the BP as the back wall flew out for the bowls game.

10) There were rousing cheers for Ann Murray when she smashed the busts!

11) Two minor points for Wardrobe and Wigs – at the final bow one of the Flunkies had no cuffs at all, and another only one. Ann Murray's wig had a loose piece which flopped when she moved her head or bowed.

I thought the show ran extremely well – flying, lighting, Wardrobe and Wigs were all wonderful. There was tumultuous applause, cheers and whistles at the end. The audience thoroughly enjoyed itself – this is definitely one of our greatest hits!

LINDA TAYLOR
Technical Administration Manager

18 Show Watch Report. Every opera is watched at least once in its run by a member of staff sitting in the audience. Notice that this show watcher records the audience response and her reaction to the show as well as the technical hitches.

HOUSE ½, HOUSE OUT, CONDS ↑↓

	MEMORY	FADE	TIME	WAIT	DELAY	REMARKS	
XF	21.7	:10	:10			PRESET ACT 3. BEHIND IRON	9.5
XF	21.8	:15	:15			O/L ACT 3 - WITH IRON OUT	9.5
XF	22	:15	:15				
XF	23	:15	:15				9.5
XF	23.3	:10	:10	TFP			
XF	23.6	:40	1:30				TFP 10.0
XF	24	:30	1:00				10.1
XF	25	:20	:20	MF			10.1
MF	25.1	:10	:10	:00		LOSE 1.49 (EGG LIGHT USPS)	
XF	26	1:00	2:00				
XF	27	:10	:10				10.5
XF	27.2	:10	:10	:10			
XF	28	:10	:10				
XF	28.2	:10	:10			VIS - WHEN CLOTH ⅔ OUT	10.2
XF	29	:30	:30				
XF	30	:30	1:00				10.4
XF	32	:08	:08			DBO EOA 3	↓
XF	33	:03	:03			1ST. CALL STATE	END 15
XF	34	:03	:03			GREEN CLOTH IN LTS	
XF	35	:10	:10				
XF	36	:07	:07				
XF	39	:05	:05			END OF SHOW DRESSING	
						EOA 3 EOS	

19 Lighting cues for Act 3. The XF and MF cues are recorded on the left. The column indicates their cue number on the computer, the next the time the cue takes to come in and the next time the previous cue takes to go out. The time between cues is recorded on the far right. The top line refers to the Front of House lighting at the beginning of the act. The House lights are reduced to half level, then turned off and the conductor's spot light is turned up and (once the applause has subsided) down.

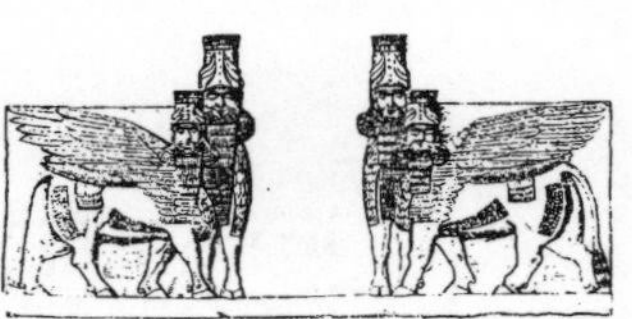

AFTERNOON ENTERTAINMENTS

HYDE PARK (AT THE COCKPIT)

p.m.	
3.0 to 3.10	Nautical Orchestra.
3.10 to 3.30	Display of Folk Dancing by a team of children from London Schools.
4.0 to 4.20	Community Singing accompanied by the Orchestra.
5.0 to 5.20	Children's Ballet.
5.20 to 5.45	Nautical Orchestra.
5.45 to 7.30	Military Band Concert with sessions of Community Singing.
7.0	Scottish Pipers and Dancers.

¶From 3 to 6 p.m. two Punch and Judy entertainments will play at hourly intervals.

HYDE PARK (BANDSTAND)

3.0 to 5.45	Salvation Army Regent Hall Band, with sessions of Community Singing.

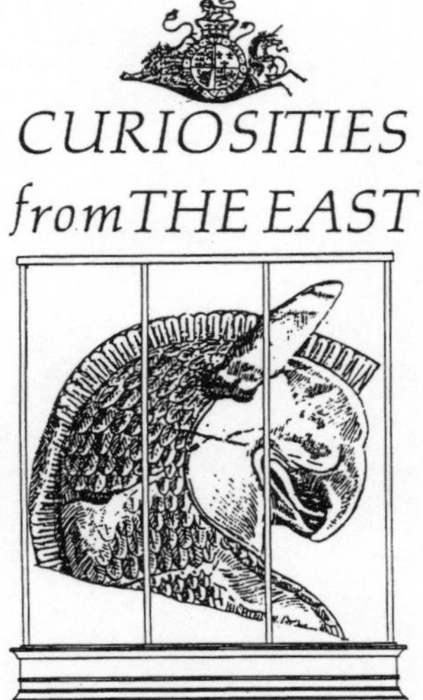

20 Programme covers carried by the cast during the show for the Concert, Investiture, Pillar and Griffin Scenes respectively.

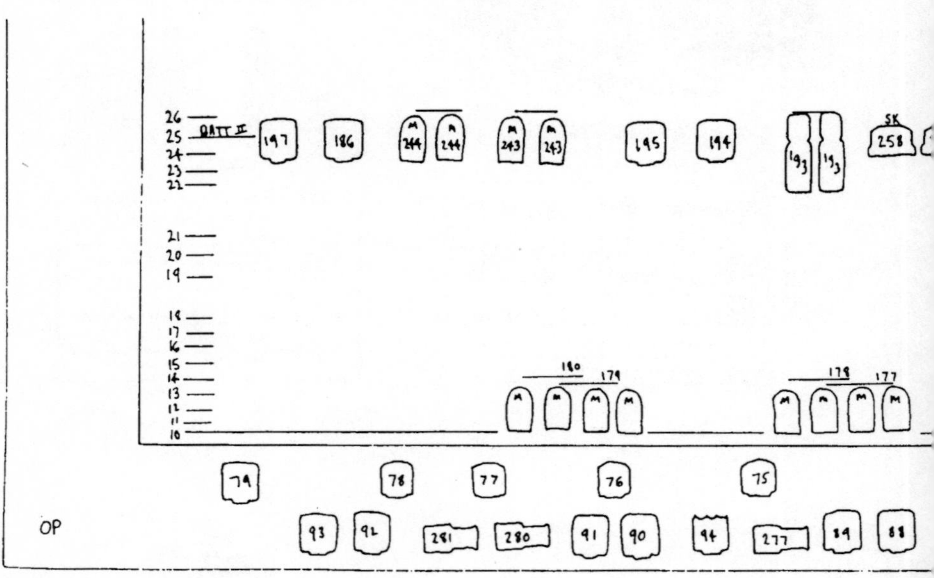

21 Part of the lighting plan for the DS area of the stage. Notice how far back the actual lighting bars start. The lamps indicated for the DS are tucked behind the Proscenium arch.

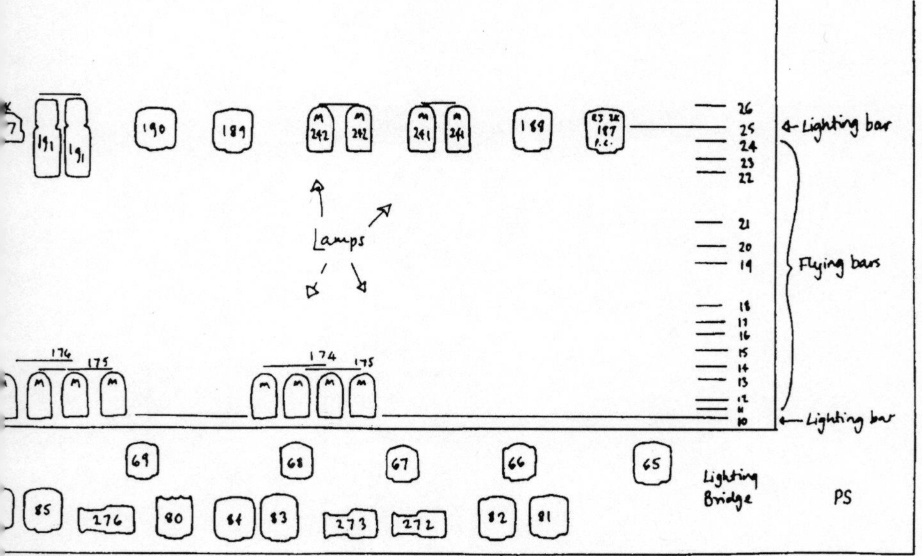
Lamps
Lighting bar
Flying bars
Lighting bar
Lighting Bridge
PS